THE PRIEST AS MANAGER

THE PRIEST
AS MANAGER

ARTHUR X. DEEGAN, II, Ph.D.

THE BRUCE PUBLISHING COMPANY / New York

427

Library of Congress Catalog Card Number: 74–76814
Copyright © 1969 The Bruce Publishing Company
Made in the United States of America

INTRODUCTION

It is important from the outset to have a clear understanding of the purpose of this book and the rationale behind the inclusion—or elimination—of the material it contains. This is a book of guidelines for the priest-manager of today. It explains principles from the science of management and endeavors to show how they are as applicable in the work of the apostolate as they are in the administration of a business enterprise, a university, an arm of the government, a military unit, or any group of men working toward a common objective.

Some priests will feel resentful of the suggestion that they are bedfellows of the materialistic "businessman" or the hardnosed "warlord." The last thing they want is to be made over to the image of mammon, spelled today G-e-n-e-r-a-l M-o-t-o-r-s. Hence they may mistakenly believe this book is not for them.

Other priests will deny the role of manager at all, understanding the post-Vatican II ideal of the priesthood to be one of brotherhood with the rest of God's people in forming a community where there is no distinction of superior-inferior, manager-managed. They, too, mistakenly may believe this book is not intended for them.

Still others will recognize their proper administrative role—after all, haven't they been exercising their stewardship for these many years now? But they would doubt very seriously whether the "tricks" of business, politics and the like can be very helpful in church work and so they also may mistakenly believe this book is not of any value to them.

A clarification of what is here meant by "manager" will enable all of the above to find at least *potential* help in the perusal of this book. The word is used in a broad sense of "a person whose duty it is to coordinate the activities of others." In this sense it is more akin to the generic word *leader* than the specific connotation of *financial steward* or *administrator of temporalities*. Manager is therefore taken in a wide sociological sense of first among equals, and not in any pejorative sense of ruler.

We may discuss *ad nauseam* today the merits and demerits of structure and bemoan the loss of individual freedom in many of the particular organizational structures known to us. But whether we do or not, the simple sociological fact of the matter is that whenever two or more people associate together to achieve an avowed goal one will become the leader and the others will become followers.

The leader may become so by being appointed to a position of responsibility; he may be elected to this position; or he may just rise to the occasion. One way or another there will be a leader and there will be followers.

This is so because in any group effort there are especially three functions which must be performed by someone: 1) someone must obtain members and keep the group intact; 2) someone must make it possible for the members to work together; 3) someone must keep the group moving toward its goals. It isn't a matter of arbitrarily deciding to build a structure and assign duties to people, one of whom we call a leader. Leadership springs up to fill the above mentioned needs.

> Leadership is a dynamic phenomenon. It is the cohesive force which holds the group intact, the accommodating factor which makes it possible for the members to live together, and the disciplinary power that keeps the unit as a whole moving toward a goal. Above all else it is a directing of followership toward objectives by meeting in a complementary, exploitative or counteractive move, the observable or anticipated actions and reactions of others.[1]

It is the same in the Church. In this religious organization, be it envisioned as the pilgrim people of God or the community that must be formed to give witness to Christ, we each have a role to play. It must be left to the theologians and bishops to determine our proper role in the final analysis under the prompting of the conciliar documents. But whatever the role of the priest turns out to be in the end, it must be somehow to be a leader, to have the responsibility for

[1] C. T. Hardwick and B. F. Landay, *Administrative Strategy* (N.Y.: Simmons-Boardman Publishing Corp., 1961), p. 23.

membership maintenance, group interaction facilitation, and objective attainment.

It is in this context then that we wish to discuss the priest as manager. We are not talking about making him into a carbon copy of the General Motors executive. We are not talking about only his role as an administrator of temporalities. We are referring to the *leadership* role to be exercised by every priest in sharing the three-fold role of the bishop—and of Christ ultimately—namely to teach, to sanctify and to serve, as he helps shape the lay person into the Christ witness which the latter must become. This will then apply to the busy urban pastor of a parish of three or four thousand families, to the hospital chaplain, to the high school counselor (or school pastor as he prefers to be called), to the assistant who runs the parish catechetical program and moderates the parish men's club.

Assuming for the moment that the priest has this leadership role, why is it desirable to read and study a book of guidelines?

Primarily because this role of leader, administrator, manager, supervisor—we use the words synonymously here—is a special profession. As an ordained clergyman the priest is already a member of one profession and shares the duties and privileges of that professional group. We are saying now that he is also a member of a second profession, that of manager, and shares with managers and all other leaders of men the duties and prerogatives of that profession.

Now, just as the priest, doctor, lawyer, teacher are expected to practice their profession according to generally accepted norms and codes, so is the manager. And just as the priest recognizes the necessity of keeping up with the latest developments, theological trends, etc. in his first profession, so should he recognize the advantages of keeping abreast of the most recent approved techniques and tools of being a manager.

Lawrence Appley, President of the American Management Association, has said that management as a profession is in about the same position today as the medical profession was in when doctors decided that working in a drug store or helping doctors was not sufficient training to be a doctor. This means that exposure to managers or helping managers is no longer considered sufficient training to be a manager. Just as was the case with the medical profession so in the priesthood for a long time it has been thought that the way to learn to be a pastor, for example, was to be exposed to pastors for a certain number of years. Through such exposure one would gradually learn to be a pastor. It was considered to be a process of osmosis.

Today we have learned that leadership training must be much more than that. And so we are witnessing a tremendous growth in manager training activities and in the use of professional management techniques. Witness the number of people who have enrolled in formal management training programs of one sort or another: from less than 10,000 a year in 1948 to an estimated 900,000 in 1968.

Not that one can be exposed to management for a day, a week, a month or even longer and come away a skilled professional manager. But given the wide exposure today of management as a science in its own right, people like priests in responsible positions of authority cannot afford to exercise leadership without serious attempts to do so according to the most up-to-date techniques of management.

It is in this light that this book hopes to achieve the following objectives:

1. A more adequate knowledge of the basic concepts of leadership, management and supervision in order to strengthen the priest's ability to coordinate the activities of others.
2. Identification and analysis of alternative styles of leadership and their connection with the problems of motivating others to contribute their part to the various works of the apostolate to which a priest might be assigned.
3. An understanding of how to change attitudes and/or supervisory skills where these require improvement.
4. An appreciation of the necessity for earning authority to give efficacy to the *formal* authority which a priest has by virtue of his priesthood.
5. Practice in using skills of communication, setting goals, solving problems, and making decisions, especially through analysis of case situations and suggested areas for discussion of some practical tasks of today's busy priests.
6. An understanding of the approach to administration known as management by objectives with an opportunity to practice setting standards for subordinates and associates and rendering meaningful appraisal of the performance of oneself and others.

If further argument be necessary for a priest to learn more about his role of manager, he would do well to consider the increased role of the layman in decision-making in the Church. As the laity take what the conciliar documents refer to as their proper role in the Church in the modern world the priest will find himself the partner of the laymen in determining directions, solving problems, making plans. In doing this he will be baring his goal-setting and decision-making processes to the scrutiny of these lay persons who may be more expert than he in such activities. Stripped of his former protection as the only one to be involved in Church decisions he will find himself having to answer to lay persons for the actions he takes. Will he not be well advised to learn what he can or what he needs to know to hold his own in his field where others may be more at home?

A final word about the possible use of this book. The various topics covered have been used as a basis for a day of recollection for priests. This was tried first as a prepastoral institute for those anticipating appointment to a pastorate in the near future. Then it was done in conjunction with the annual retreat giving all priests in the diocese the opportunity of at least a basic introduction to management. While this book is not intended to be a "textbook" in the classical sense, it is being used as the core matter for a leadership training course in a seminary. This is in response to the suggestion of many priests that these matters be made a part of a cleric's training early in his career rather than after he has tried to find the answer to some of these problems on his own for many years.

And finally it is hoped that the guidelines suggested here might even provide interesting bedtime (or other) reading for the busy priest who may not be fortunate enough to have the opportunity to join a study group to discuss these principles, but who nonetheless wishes to avail himself of a not-too-formidable introductory text on the mysterious world of management.

CONTENTS

THE PRIEST AS MANAGER

CHAPTER ONE

THE PROCESS OF MANAGEMENT

For the benefit of the reader who makes it a practice never to read the introduction to a book, it will be advisable to say here that we use the words manager, leader, administrator, and supervisor interchangeably. The essence of the managerial role we have in mind is "the coordination of the activities of others."

Other definitions are to be found in management literature. Perhaps the most common is "to get things done through people." To this basic definition it might be useful to add the word "voluntarily." Otherwise some very strange people would qualify as managers. Take Jesse James for instance: he was able to "get things done through people" all right. Indeed, every time he got on a train and walked down the aisle with an open burlap sack he got people to toss money, watches, jewelry, and the like into his sack. Only incidentally, he held a gun to their head!

Perhaps one of the most insightful definitions of management to be found today is given by Harold Koontz, Professor of Management at the Graduate School of Business Administration, University of California, at Los Angeles. He says that the manager is primarily an environment creator; his job is to design and operate an environment where people, working together in groups, contribute toward the attainment of group purposes.

In the context of the role of a priest, then, he must seek to provide the climate of environment for the rest of us to exercise our proper role in bearing witness to Christ. He must make it possible for us to recognize our duties and our rights. He must make it easier for us to find our way as pilgrims to our heavenly destiny. His is a facilitating contribution to our eternal salvation.

Job of Manager—A Distinct Job

Every young supervisor who has worked his way up through the ranks to a supervisory position has experienced the difficulty of trying to explain to others how his supervisory job is different from his non-supervisory work. Maybe he was a top flight accountant or skilled machine operator or successful salesman. And because he was so good in his particular line, his qualifications were recognized by someone in higher authority and he was promoted to be the chief accountant or foreman of the machine operators or sales supervisor as the case might be. Too often, however, in announcing to his family and acquaintances that he had received such a promotion, he was hard put to explain how what he did now was different from what he was doing before. Very often his attempts at explanation ended rather abruptly in a simple pronouncement that "I'm the boss."

When pressed further for detailed explanation, the young supervisor often resorts to an explanation of the work that his newly acquired subordinates are supposed to be doing and over which he does have supervisory responsibility but which do not make up his daily duties. In reality the supervisor's job consists of those things that he must do in order that the functions of his subordinates can be carried out to their proper conclusion. And in this sense he obviously must not do the same things as his subordinates, but serve a facilitative function which makes it possible for them to achieve their goals.

Dr. Earl Strong, Professor of Management at Pennsylvania State University, uses the figure on page 33 to show the distinction between the job of a supervisor or manager and the work of followers in the group. He suggests that an analogy might be drawn between these two distinctive types of work in any kind of organization and the distinct functions of the two wheels on a bicycle. Looking at the figure, and ignoring for a moment the words that label different elements of the picture, the question might be asked: which of the two wheels in a bicycle is more important? Consideration of this question will generally lead to the immediate conclusion that both wheels of the bicycle are necessary if the bicycle is to serve its proper function, namely transporting the rider from one place to another. However, even after admitting that both wheels are necessary, that both

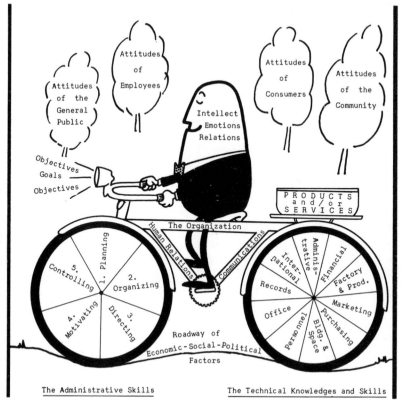

Attitudes of the General Public

Attitudes of Employees

Attitudes of Consumers

Attitudes of the Community

Intellect
Emotions
Relations

Objectives
Goals
Objectives

PRODUCTS
and/or
SERVICES

The Organization

Human Relations
Communications

1. Planning
2. Organizing
3. Directing
4. Motivating
5. Controlling

Administrative
International
Financial
Factory & Prod.
Marketing
Purchasing
Bldg. & Space
Personnel
Office
Records

Roadway of
Economic-Social-Political
Factors

The Administrative Skills

The Technical Knowledges and Skills

FIGURE 1

Reprinted from *The Management of Business: An Introduction,* by Earl P. Strong. Harper and Row (1965), Figure 1, p. 10. By permission of author and publisher.

must be in proper operating order if the bicycle is to be of use to the rider, we can still ask which of the two wheels is the more important.

First answers will often choose in favor of the rear wheel. It is felt that the rear wheel is the one which provides the push, the drive, the motion and which thereby makes it possible for the bike to go. Further reflection, however, will normally lead to the rejoinder: "but what good is the propelling push or drive from the rear wheel if all this drive accomplishes is propelling the bicycle and its driver into the nearest telephone pole?" Obviously, it is necessary that the proper function of the front wheel come into play; that is, the front wheel must guide and channel the activity and motion provided by the spinning of the rear wheel. And for the overall objective of the bicycle getting from one place to another predetermined place, perhaps it is convincing to argue that the front wheel provides the more important of the two functions. (It is for this reason that the diagram cheats a little bit by not showing the chain connecting the pedals to the rear wheel.)

While all analogies limp, and therefore while it is recognized that this bicycle example is not entirely compelling, still with regard to the distinction between the two kinds of work it is clear that each wheel will perform a separate function.

Look now at the words which label the various elements of the figure. It is suggested that this is a picture of the typical organization or group of people, be it business enterprise or other human organization responsible for providing a product or service to the community. It can be seen that there are two distinct types of skills necessary on the part of the various personnel who make up the organization. The rear wheel enumerates the various technical knowledge and skills and functions which take place at the worker level in an organization. These are the people who provide the hustle and bustle of activity in the organization. They perform the manifold activities that are necessary in order to make the group go as it were.

On the other hand the front wheel symbolizes those skills and functions which must take place at a different level in the organization if all of the hustle and bustle from the rear wheel is to achieve the group's objectives. The frame, of course, indicates that the organization as a whole keeps these two kinds of functions united, especially with the help of the A-frame of human relations and communications. Further it is evident that only when all of these elements together are present can the product and/or services of the organization be supported in the market basket.

To complete the explanation of the figure: it takes the intellect, emotions and various relationships as perceived by human beings (the rider) to move the bicycle placidly over the roadway of economic, social and political factors through the atmosphere that is provided by the attitudes of the general public, the employees, the consumers, and the community at large.

The lesson here might very well be: managers must learn to get off

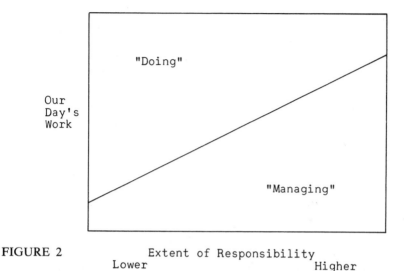

FIGURE 2

the rear wheel and start riding the front wheel if the organization is to achieve its purposes.

Is this distinction between the kind of work performed by a leader and the kind of work performed by followers helpful for the priest in carrying out his leadership responsibilities? Perhaps this can be answered by referring to Figure 2. It will be noted that the X axis, or bottom line, of the figure measures extent of responsibility in an organization; and the Y axis, or vertical line, measures our day's work. The figure shows us first of all that if we examine our day's work we will probably find that it can conveniently be broken up into two general types of activities: one might be labeled technical, or busy kind of work, the sort that was symbolized by the rear wheel of our bicycle; and the second, managerial work as enumerated on the spokes of the front wheel of our bicycle. The figure suggests that as one moves along the line on the bottom from the low ranks of managerial responsibility to the higher ranks of managerial responsibility something happens to the daily activities of the people who hold these respective positions. To make this somewhat concrete, think for a moment of an organization such as the typical diocese. At the upper end the person who has the broadest managerial responsibility for the entire diocese would be, of course, the Ordinary. As you go down the line of managerial responsibility you go through chancellors and deans with their responsibilities, to the parish where we have the pastor with prime responsibility for this smaller segment of the diocese; and within the parish down through the assistant priest and even to the person who might be delegated president or leader of a specific parish organization or activity. At that level we probably have the lowest rank of responsibility for official organizational work within a diocese.

The diagonal line in the figure separates the way in which we might look at the things each of these people does in carrying out his managerial responsibilities. What this tells us is that if we have a person at the left end—the president of a parish organization—he has only a minimum amount of managerial responsibilities and quite an amount of technical or vocational responsibilities. He is more involved with doing the things that must be done in an organization, whatever it happens to be, and less involved in making decisions, in doing the planning and controlling the operations of the overall organization, namely the diocese. As we move on to the right, perhaps halfway or three-quarters of the way along, we come to a pastor who has considerably more managerial responsibilities and considerably fewer vocational or occupational responsibilities. He divides his day's time approximately that way.

As we go over to the very right hand extreme with the Ordinary, one would say that he spends almost all his time on managerial activities and only a very minimum amount (perhaps none at all) in a technical vocational occupation.

What the figure tells us, then, is that as one takes on managerial responsibilities, he is supposed to shed his vocational cloak, using the term vocation in the sense of technical and not, of course, sacerdotal, work. The problem encountered, however—and this is true in churches, in schools, in hospitals, in business—time after time is that people cling to their vocational, or occupational, practices. There is a special nickname given this in the literature: it is called clinging to "occupational hobbies." It seems that as people take on additional managerial responsibilities they like to keep themselves involved in the things they used to do before they became managers or supervisors at whatever level. They like to continue doing whatever they were called upon to do before.

An example in the business world would be the man who has been an assistant foreman—the fellow who is always responsible for fixing the machine in a maintenance department—who gets a promotion. He becomes supervisor of the whole department. One fine day the machine breaks down, and when he is told about it, he hears the news with glee. He hasn't rolled up his sleeves and gotten grease on his hands for a long time. So he decides to drop the important planning he is doing and reverts, as it were, to his earlier occupation. He may spend six or seven hours trying to fix the machine while important papers pile up on his desk, or phone calls come in that he can't answer, or people try to see him without success because he is busy in an "occupational hobby." He has forgotten that as a manager he is supposed to delegate this job to somebody else: he is not supposed to be doing it himself anymore.

Or take a parish: here is a man who was an assistant for many years and was used to mailing out notices for meetings or calling up important lay people in the parish to arrange for a meeting, and other similar tasks. Now he is a pastor. And he decides one day as a pastor that it is time to have a meeting of certain folks, so he tells his secretary to arrange for such a meeting. But he doesn't stop there because he used to do this sort of thing himself and knows all the details of it. He knows whom to call and how to call or what kind of a note to send out and how soon in advance to send it and all the rest. So he spends an hour telling Susie Jones in the front office what to say in a little note, how large a sheet of paper to use, exactly what time to mail it, who the people are that ought to be relied upon to contact other people, and so on and so forth. He might spend an hour doing this when he could have delegated it in two minutes; but he spends the time doing it because he used to do it himself and nobody could do it as he did it, after all. He forgets that in his new role he is supposed to shed this "occupational hobby" that he used to have and occupy his time with the important things that have to be done as administrator.

The lesson, then, is that to become an administrator, to become a leader or a manager in the religious field or any other, requires what might be called a small sacrifice. It requires the avoidance of the temptation to get involved in the details, the minutiae of the things that one was accustomed to doing before being given additional responsibilities. And sometimes that is a sacrifice because it is difficult to force oneself to sit behind a desk, or get on the telephone, or do the "people" kind of work. There are those of us who just do not like "people" work. We much prefer to roll up our sleeves and do the dirty work ourselves. This, however, is the change that must take place when taking on higher additional managerial responsibilities.

The priest must learn that instead of being occupied with the *how* (as for example, this pastor who told how to get the meeting together), he should spend time being occupied with the *what*. He makes the decisions, he does the planning, he decides what has to be done, and then has someone else get it done. That is the difference between being a manager and being a vocation, or occupation, holder.

The Functions of a Manager

Let us now turn to a description in some detail of what is meant by each of the five managerial functions that were enumerated around the spokes of the front wheel of our bicycle. It will be recalled that the five management functions are: planning, organizing, directing, motivating, and controlling. As such they are thought to be generally applicable to all leaders or managers at whatever level of responsibility in whatever type of organization one might have.

1. Planning

The *planning* function pertains to the steps taken in developing programs and in determining means to implement these programs, in pursuit of chosen objectives, whose determination is also a part of the planning process. In this regard planning involves the study of the future and the completion of the series of courses of action. Planning is hard work in that it demands the intensive use of the manager's mental capacities. Because of its difficulties, planning is all too often the one function which is "short changed." The self-styled activist believes that the time it takes to plan his actions is wasted, and he foolishly "rushes in where angels fear to tread." Henry Fayol, a management pioneer, said the "preparation of a plan of action is one of the most difficult and most important matters of every business and brings into play all departments and all functions, especially the management functions."

The scope of planning is organization-wide: it includes the determination of all long-run objectives, the dedication to a particular philosophy, the formulation of principles which will govern the activities of the organization, the statement of policies which are defined as guides for decision-making on the part of other persons in the organization as well as detailed procedures for step-by-step carrying out of program activities in the pursuit of short-run goals or objectives.

Planning for a priest might include the preparations for construction of a church, the scheduling of masses, the drawing up of by-laws for a parish organization, various kinds of rules and regulations governing conduct of educational activities in the parish, determination of priorities for the allocation of monetary resources and the like.

2. Organizing

After plans have been developed, *organizing* is next in order. This function is concerned with the enumeration of activities to be carried out if the goals are to be achieved, the grouping of these activities into coherent and cohesive categories, the procurement of necessary personnel to carry out the plans, the designing of systems of interaction of these sub-units of the organization, the establishment of lines of communication among the various parties involved, and the assignment of clearly determined authority and responsibility to each person especially at the supervisory level.

This is often facilitated by the formation of an organization structure diagrammed on what is called an organization chart. Such a chart is a picture of the relationship that exists between the various units of the organization. It depicts each unit in its proper place, clearly indicating authority relationships and channels of communication.

Finally, organizing also includes providing each person with the physical facilities and equipment resources necessary for the accomplishment of his assigned tasks.

3. Directing

Directing refers to the function of running the organization units responsible for carrying out specific plans. It involves day by day supervision of the way people carry out their assigned tasks. It includes such things as giving instructions to people in detailed requirements for the proper performance of their operations, training people in the proper methods of carrying out their duties, giving instructions to personnel regarding actions deemed necessary by the manager, and coordinating all the activities of all the units under one's jurisdiction.

4. Motivating

The fourth function, *motivating*, is closely connected with directing. It may be defined technically as "the integration of personal objectives with the primary service objectives of the organization," or more prosaically "getting people to *want* to do the things that you want them to do."

Methods for getting people to do their job have run the gamut over the years from emphasis on monetary and other personal reward incentives to the current behavioral science emphasis upon need satisfaction in the carrying out of one's duty.

Professor Frederick Herzberg, Chairman of the Psychology Department at Case Western Reserve University, poses the question, "What is the simplest, surest and most direct way of getting someone to do something?" He then answers his own question as follows:

> Ask him? But if he responds that he does not want to do it then that calls for a psychological consultation to determine the reasons for his obstinancy. Tell him? But if his response shows that he does not understand you, now an expert in communications methods has to be brought in to show you how to get through to him. Give him a monetary incentive? I do not need to remind the reader of the complexity and difficulty involved in setting up and administering an incentive system. Show him? This means a costly training program. We need a simple way.[1]

This suggests the complexities involved in answering the question of motivation for employees who are paid to do a job. The fact that most of the followers of the priest-manager receive no monetary remuneration for their work, makes the task of motivation even more involved. Because of the danger of a follower leaving the organization if he does not find in it satisfaction for the purposes for which he joined, it is even more important that the priest-leader be expert in integrating the individual's personal goals and desires with the objective of the entire group. In this sense his most frequent motivational problem concerns curtailing activities on the part of individuals when they might jeopardize programs of the entire group. Thus he seeks an answer to the question: how do you keep people interested in your program and willing to contribute their talents to it when they cannot operate the way they themselves would like to?

[1] Frederick Herzberg, "One More Time: How Do You Motivate Employees?" *Harvard Business Review* (Jan.-Feb. 1968), p. 54.

5. Controlling

The fifth managerial function, *controlling*, concerns the threefold task of recording results of performance, measuring these results against original plans, and initiating needed corrective measures. Controlling is then a regulative function of management and may take any of several forms. Regulatory devices used include budgetary controls, standard operating procedures, quality control specifications, standards of performance, and all sorts of reporting measures. Regulation may be oral, written, or a combination of both.

The connection between controlling and planning ought to be evident. Planning involves the original determination of what is desired by way of performance; controlling consists of checking to see that original plans are carried out and determining to what extent this is possible.

Need for Modern Priests To Be Effective Managers

The Church today is undergoing severe pressure from both within and without to put her operations on a "more businesslike basis." This means that the priest who is a manager must perform the above managerial functions on a "more businesslike basis." What is usually meant by this phrase? It has something to do with being able to achieve results. The results may not necessarily be measured in dollars of profit, nor in accolades, but in success in achieving organizational objectives. In other words, priests must become effective in their roles of leading others.

Research has shown that, unlike other managers, Catholic priests advance to positions of responsibility as pastors rather on a basis of seniority than of proven managerial ability.[2] This research verified that excellence in performing the functions of the professional cleric did not serve as a determining factor in promotion to positions of authority as a pastor. Had this been the case it might be conceivable to argue that spiritual performance is after all more directly related to the overall purposes of the organization and that administrator-managerial abilities are strictly secondary.

[2] Cf. T. R. O'Donovan and A. X. Deegan, "Some Career Determinants of Church Executives," *Sociology and Social Research*, Vol. 48, No. 1 (Oct. 1963), and "A Comparative Study of the Orientation of a Selected Group of Church Executives," *Sociology and Social Research*, Vol. 48, No. 4 (Apr. 1964).

Pastors and administrators today are called upon to exercise the usual management functions as part of their responsibility in overseeing multimillion dollar physical plants. Annual budgets range anywhere from $250,000 to over $1,000,000; religious and social activities often involve organizations whose members sometimes number over 10,000.

A large part of the present Catholic Church modernization, at least in our country, concerns the acclimating of the pastor's apostolic spirit to the exigency of an industrialized society. It is society that is changed and the Church must meet the new man who is the product of this society. Society is no longer predominantly rural; modern man is urban. Industrialization has changed society completely and the work of science is going to accomplish a still greater transformation in the years to come. The Church especially in its basic unit, the local parish, will have to make major adaptations, because the parish, more than any other part of the Church structure, will feel the effects of the new conditions.

These new conditions have been the object of sociological study for several decades. But little attention has been paid to the consequent need for structural changes and/or research into managerial patterns of priests. They are thus left to their own devices to face staggering responsibilities. For example, the parish of today is the only unit in the Church which is totally supported by free will offerings. All others receive at least part of their funds from fixed fees, tuition, or charges of one sort or other. This means that the parish priest bears the sole responsibility for raising and spending his annual budget, bereft of the aids available to institutional administrators.

Lest this argument be misconstrued as a plea for what has come to be known as the "efficiency-expert" approach, it would be helpful to distinguish between *efficiency* and *effectiveness*. The dictionary defines "efficiency" as the ability to do things without waste of time, energy, etc; a quality possessed by one who is effective. On the other hand, "effective" is defined as producing the desired effect; efficient. Fowler states that both effective and efficient mean having effect, but with different applications and certain often disregarded shades of meaning.[3]

"Efficient" is said to apply to agents or their action and means

[3] *Fowler's Modern English Usage* (New York: Oxford University Press, 1940), p. 128.

"capable of producing the desired effect, not incompetent or unequal to a task." On the other hand, "effective" applies to the things done or to its doer as such and means "having a high degree of effect." The apparent minor differences in these two definitions have significant differences in connotation which can be helpful and prevent the misinterpretation that could arise here.

> Efficiency implies action with a minimum of waste. The efficient factory worker for example is the one who goes through the motions of his job operation without waste motion. Similarly the efficient manager is one whose activity involves no waste of time or effort.

> Effectiveness relates to results achieved. The effective ball player for example is the one who has the best batting average at the end of the season. The effective executive likewise is the one who scores high when you rate him on the basis of results achieved.[4]

Because of this difference in connotation, it is possible to be efficient and not effective; for example, one could do the right things without the waste of time or motion, but get no results. On the other hand, it is possible to be effective and not efficient; for example, one might get results at the cost of the morale of subordinates.

What is the major problem? It is fundamentally the confusion between effectiveness and efficiency that stands between doing the right things and doing things right. There is surely nothing quite so useless as doing with great efficiency what should not be done at all.[5]

Practices of an Effective Manager

Determining who is effective and who is not, then, means determining who is getting results and who is not. Ways of measuring this vary considerably. In one research endeavor, five specific criteria for measuring effectiveness were determined as a result of breaking down the job of the priest, especially the pastor, into five rather arbitrary component parts as follows:

1. Area of financial administration: is the pastor able to raise and handle funds in such a way that the parish can build the necessary buildings and pay off the debt according to the potential in his area? Does the pastor maintain the standard accounts

[4] Auren Uris, *The Efficient Executive* (New York: McGraw-Hill Book Co., 1957), p. 299.
[5] Peter Drucker, "Managing for Business Effectiveness," *Harvard Business Review,* May-June 1963.

and accounting reports for the diocese as he should? Does the pastor cooperate in diocesan campaigns according to the potential in his area?

2. Human relations area: is the pastor able to administer to the parish effectively (get results) and yet not forget the human dignity of the assistant pastors, employees, and parishioners? Measure the pastor by any interpersonal problems he might have had with the assistant pastors, complaints from clergy, or laity, or his overall general reputation for handling people as known generally in the diocese.

3. General administrative capacity: does the pastor have a reputation for completing assignments on schedule, meeting deadlines, getting in reports, carrying out projects, being punctual and thorough?

4. Attitude of cooperation regarding superiors: does the pastor strive to carry out in his parish all diocesan directives, policies, projects, as a member of a larger team?

5. Self improvement area: does the pastor seek to improve his own knowledge and skills in administrative-pastoral matters? Does he attend conferences, initiate study programs, seek professional advancement?

If this is the way in which one might measure effectiveness, there is still the matter of how one learns to become effective.

What is the difference between a manager who is effective and one who is not? Over the years successful managers develop their own individual formulae for success. Attempting to synthesize what many successful managers have found, management consultant Peter Drucker defines the effective executive as the one who has acquired a degree of competence in certain basic practices which are said to be deceptively simple, yet exceedingly hard to do well. He identifies five such practices or habits of the mind:

1. Effective executives know where their time goes.
2. Effective executives focus on outward contribution.
3. Effective executives build on strength.
4. Effective executives concentrate on the few major areas where superior performance will produce outstanding results.
5. Effective executives make effective decisions.[6]

[6] Peter Drucker, *The Effective Executive* (New York: Harper & Row, 1967).

Each of these practices is discussed at length in one of the succeeding chapters. Chapter Three deals entirely with the difficulty of improving the use of one's time, which is the first practice of an effective executive. Chapter Six, on the managerial system known as Management by Objectives, deals specifically with the second, third, and fourth of Drucker's practices of effectiveness. Chapter Seven treats of the final practice of effectiveness, namely, the ability to make effective decisions.

CHAPTER TWO

DEVELOPMENT OF MANAGEMENT THEORY

As a formal science or body of knowledge, management theory is still in the embryonic stage. As with any nascent science, it is only through long years of arduous work in hypothesizing and proving or disproving hypotheses that we will be able someday to have a neatly indexed set of facts to serve as rules for the functions of management. Meanwhile, however, it will be useful to examine what is presently advanced in management thought.

The present position of management thought is best understood in the light of previous beliefs. So in order to better understand current trends in management theory, we should first study the history of management.

Definition of Terms

A *history* is too often considered to be the study of archaic events or ideas which may have been important to someone somewhere at some time, but which have no value for the present except as museum pieces. It must be understood that the history here considered is by no means of this type of antiquated information. Management theory is too dynamic for that. All of the ideas and principles we shall study have meaning not only for their own time but for the present as well. Almost all the important contributions to management theory which have preceded our time have had a deep influence on our era and continue to effect our thought. Our history, then, must be considered as a study of the past in an attempt to explain the present.

Management as used in this chapter has a dual meaning. In the broad sense, management is the body of thoughts or principles to be used as guides of action taken by managers. In the limited sense, it refers to the action performed by managers in accordance with these principles, which action we have defined in the last chapter as "co-ordinating the activities of others."

Hence, a history of management is a study of various principles which have been adhered to as the rationale used by those whose function it is to direct the activities of others and thus get done the things which get done in this world of ours.

Management Literature and the History of Management

Most management authors speak of the history of management as the evolution of a body of management principles. They recount various theories and/or hypotheses advanced, and arbitrarily codify them into time periods for the purpose of easy identification. They trace the progress of management theory from the era of Scientific Management (1880–1930) through the period of Human Relations (1930–1950) to the present-day Quantitative and Behaviorist champions (1950 to date). Or they aptly name the periods after various individuals who were the most articulate in proposing their theories during the period in which they lived. Thus, they refer to the period of Frederick W. Taylor, or the Elton Mayo period, etc. Each of these terms and periods shall be explained shortly.

While maintaining these traditional concepts, the present writer does not believe they constitute a true evolution of management theory, in the sense of an interrelated series of developments, such that each successive one evolved from the previous one. Rather, changes in management theory have been brought about by external stimuli, mainly by the different economic stresses of society. Working man is a social animal, and his outlook on proper management will be colored, even dominated, by the social system and economic structure in which he lives. Hence, management theory has undergone the same changes as has society's sharing of the earth's wealth.

One of the first corollaries of an economic system is the concept of authority vested in the political head and in the managers on various economic levels. And authority is so important a property of management that whatever the outlook toward authority is, such will be the outlook on management as a whole. Indeed the history of management might also be considered a history of authority, for within any society there are the governing and the governed, the ruling and the ruled, the managing and the managed. If the framework of the state's power and authority is highly centralized and autocratic, the rationale of the business management will probably be equally highly centralized. If, on the other hand, the ruling body is built on more liberal principles, the views of management will also probably be broader.

Following this position, i.e., that we are actually examining the history of authority, we find the following arbitrary division into periods of reference, based on the economic structures of the time: Period I—from the beginning of man's cooperative effort to the end of the 18th century; Period II—the 19th century to the end of the 1920's; Period III—from the end of the 1920's to the present.

First Period—To the End of the 18th Century

a. Social system background. This would be the period of complete domination of the workers by their supervisors, based on a social caste system of autocracy. This was the society of the ancient Egyptians, where the whip and the ball-and-chain were literally the only techniques of management in building pyramids. An effective way to get things done through people! This was also the society of the Roman Empire where the fact of being a citizen of Rome separated the managers from all other men (barbarians) and the Roman Legion was an effective technique of coordinating the activities of others! This was the society which saw the development of the Roman Catholic Church, whose central control type of government-management is only today being questioned as the most appropriate way of ruling. This was the feudal system society where landowners needed no other principles to guide their management of the serfs but their hereditary title.

This was, in fine, the society of terrible extremes: the lord and the peasant, the emperor and the slave, the knight and the foot soldier, the haves and the have-nots.

b. Management theory. In an economic system of this type it was not necessary to study an organized body of management principles. It was not necessary to do anything but be in a position of authority, for authority meant effective control, given the inequalities which obtained. These were the days of empire builders. Men were content with their lot. They were born into it, knew nothing of the world beyond it, aspired to nothing except continuing in it. It was a time when everything took ages to accomplish. The French and English fought a 100 years war. Cathedrals were built in a matter of centuries. There were attempts to build what we call guilds, or groups of craftsmen engaged in the same types of work, which have been weakly mentioned as the forerunners of latter-day trade unions; but these were of minor consequence in the social system in which they were buried. For their influence was not felt beyond the limits of the village in which they existed. Only the struggle to survive seemed to matter.

Not until men began to think beyond the realm of their immediate ken, to envision hopes of seeing in their day improvements in speed of communication, production, acquisition of wealth, etc., was it necessary to look elsewhere for effective management. This began to happen after the settlement of the New World. The Dark Ages were over. And so the first period closed as a pair of Frenchmen named Voltaire and Rousseau were popularizing the idea of fraternity, liberty and equality, and calling for a revolution in the field of politics, an enlightenment in the field of intellectual thought, and a renaissance in the field of art; and an American named Franklin was writing about "taxation without representation."

It will be noted that no study is here made of contributions of such organizations as political bodies (the Roman senate), military units (the Napoleonic army), Church hierarchies (the Roman Catholic Church) and others to the development of management concepts. Suffice it to say that they practiced management in accordance with the prevalent idea of authority at that time. While it must be recognized that they practiced certain functions of management, and originated some of the same principles we find used today, we are unable to find any codification of such principles in this period.

Second Period—The 19th Century Through the 1920's

a. Social system background. This was the period of the emergence of the working man as a unit of labor, an individual rather than a part of the chain gang. This was brought about as a result of the republics born in the western world through the American Revolution, the French Revolution, and the breakdown of the great European colonial powers, together with the development of the capitalistic form of economy. This was the society which saw agrarian reform and the redistribution of the great estates into small tracts of land with individual farmers learning the meaning of ownership. This was the society which permitted the rise of the business baron and the industrial revolution where the concept of a wage being paid for work (rather than a subsistence allowance) was recognized. This was the society where the doctrine of private property could be extolled by a Leo XIII, so the idea of collective bargaining could be born as an effective means of coordinating the activities of others.

b. Management theory. With the transition in the 1880's of the United States from a predominantly agricultural country to an industrial nation, the ideas of this new republic began to permeate management. As industrialization progressed, the unilateral authority of management gave ground to the claims of legislating governments and collective bargaining unions. The dictatorial autocracy of before became a "constitutional management" in which wages and conditions of employment are based upon laws, contracts or procedural agreements.

> And in rare cases, a system of industrial democracy may be established in which management and labor not only share in the rule-making process but also cooperate in improving efficiency and increasing output. We have called this "democratic-participative" management. In a very real sense, therefore, management-labor relations may become less authoritarian and more democratic with the advance of industrialization.[1]

This was, then, first of all the period in which labor unions became accepted as spokesmen for the workers in their dealings with management, and governments were acknowledged to have the right to legislate in order to prevent abuses either to managers or workers.

Scientific Management

Industrialization can be described as the process whereby a nation learns to create more material things through the efforts of fewer workers. The emphasis is therefore on the methods of production. A search is made for ways to effect more efficiency, correct inequities and save waste. As the United States became overrun by the Industrial Revolution, and standardization of production through the assembly-

[1] Frederick Harbison and Charles A. Myers, *Management in the Industrial World* (New York: McGraw-Hill, 1959), p. 119.

line technique, etc., management literature centered on industrial technology as the focal point of good organization.

The foremost exponent of this approach was the "father of scientific management," Frederick W. Taylor. In his work, *Scientific Management*, he promulgated a series of principles based on first-hand studies of manufacturing practices at the shop level, excoriating managers for their arbitrary approach to their responsibilities, and workers for their apparent lackadaisical attitude to work norms. Taylor recommended making management a science, resting on "well recognized, clearly defined and fixed principles, instead of depending on more or less hazy ideas."[2]

By maximizing the productive efficiency of each worker, scientific management would also maximize the earnings of workers and employers. The aim was to use all available resources and knowledge of the universe in order to realize definite ideals.

> It becomes the duty of those on the management's side to deliberately study the character, the nature, and the performance of each workman with a view to finding out his limitations on the one hand, but even more important, his possibilities for development on the other hand; and then, as deliberately and systematically to train and help and teach this workman, giving him, wherever possible, those opportunities for advancement which will finally enable him to do the highest and most interesting and most profitable class of work for which his natural abilities fit him, and which are open to him in the particular company in which he is employed.

> First, the development of the science, i.e., the gathering in on the part of those on the management's side, of all knowledge which in the past has been kept in the heads of the workmen; second, the scientific selection and progressive development of the workmen; third, the bringing of the science and the scientifically selected and trained men together; and fourth, the constant and intimate cooperation which always occurs between the men on the management's side and the workmen.[3]

Because Taylor's work was shop-oriented, including many studies of ways to increase output at the level of the individual worker, he was criticized as being a mere glorified "time-study" analyst, so much

[2] F. W. Taylor, "Shop Management," reprinted in *Scientific Management* (New York: Harper & Brothers, 1947), p. 63.
[3] Testimony before the Special House Committee, reprinted in *Scientific Management* (New York: Harper & Brothers, 1947).

so that he was called before a U.S. Special House Committee investigating the principles of the scientific management school. Before this committee, he defended his ideas as

> . . . not a piecework system, not a bonus system, not time-study. . . . The great revolution that takes place in the mental attitude of the two parties under scientific management is that both sides take their eyes off the division of the surplus as the all-important matter, and together turn their attention toward increasing the size of the surplus until this surplus becomes so large . . . that there is ample room for a large increase in wages for the workmen and an equally large increase in profits for the manufacturer.
>
> (Increased output would be so large that all frictions between employers and workers would be eliminated. It also makes collective bargaining unnecessary.)
>
> Under scientific management arbitrary power, arbitrary decision, ceases; and every single subject, large and small, becomes the question for scientific investigation, for reduction to law.[4]

Taylor thus eliminated the personal exercise of authority. Managers became subject to rules and discipline as much as the workers. It was the task of management to place the right worker in any given job, but according to scientific selection, eliminating guesswork. Arbitrary judgments of both workers and managers gave place to tests; the science of each track and both sides' willingness to abide by the laws.

It is the writer's opinion that Taylor's contribution has been somewhat overemphasized. First of all, the originality of his ideas has become suspect.[5] Further, business managers opposed the idea of replacing judgment and executive decision with prefabricated techniques. They would have nothing to do with his "mental revolution." On the whole, they accepted many of his techniques, but accused him of unwarranted interference in the domain of managerial prerogatives.[6]

Other analysts whose contributions were analogous to Taylor's included Henri Fayol, who popularized the universality of management

---

[4] F. W. Taylor's testimony before the Special House Committee to Investigate The Taylor and Other Systems of Shop Management, reprinted in *Scientific Management* (New York: Harper & Brothers, 1947).

[5] See J. H. Hoagland, "Management Before Frederick Taylor." Proceedings of the Academy of Management (1956), pp. 15–24 and unpublished dissertation of same author, ch. IX, "Influence and Significance of Charles Babbage."

[6] Robert Franklin Hoxie, *Scientific Management and Labor* (New York: D. Appleton and Company, 1915).

principles[7]; Edward D. Jones, who stressed the trusteeship role of management[8]; Frank and Lillian Gilbreth, who sought to improve the welfare of the workers[9]; Henry L. Gantt, who pursued the establishment of habits in industry[10]; and Harrington Emerson, who championed standardization.[11]

All of these furthered the cause of scientific management in order to find compatibility between management and workers.

> The mutuality of interests objective, based heavily on the economic motives of employers, was to result from ever increasing productivity and wider, more equitable distribution of an economic surplus. The pioneers felt that if this more immediate goal could be accomplished, the more ultimate necessity of human collaboration in industry would be forthcoming.[12]

To summarize, this was the period of great advance in management practice by the application of empirical studies to determine ever speedier methods of production. But it was a one-sided study. Stress was given to changes in material things for the sole purpose of improving production with little thought to the improvement of the worker, or even to his basic well-being. This could have been the only other period needed. Had it not been for the abuses which developed, this could have eventually become a period of true liberty for the individual. But abuses were there because technological advances were too rapid for the social sciences and greed was stronger than justice.

> As the art of manufacture improves, the artisan recedes; as the masses are lowered, the masters are raised; and no human bond exists between employers and employed. This indictment of industrial civilization . . . became the major theme in the lifework of Karl Marx.[13]

[7] Henri Fayol, *General and Industrial Administration* (London: Sir Isaac Pitman and Sons Ltd., 1949).

[8] Edward D. Jones, *Industrial Leadership and Executive Ability* (New York: The Engineering Magazine Co., 1920).

[9] L. M. Gilbreth, *The Psychology of Management* (New York: Sturgis and Walton Co., 1914).

[10] Henry L. Gantt, *Work, Wages and Profits* (New York: The Engineering Magazine Co., 1920).

[11] Harrington Emerson, *The Twelve Principles of Efficiency* (New York: The Engineering Magazine Co., 1912).

[12] William G. Scott, *The Social Ethic in Management Literature* (Atlanta: Georgia State College of Business Administration, 1959), p. 18.

[13] Reinhard Bendix, *Work and Authority in Industry* (New York: John Wiley & Sons, 1956), p. xviii.

So the period had to be purged, unfortunately by the unholy cry, "workers of the world, unite" . . . which culminated in the emergence of the socialistic state through the Russian Revolution in 1917.

Third Period—From 1920's to the Present

a. *Social background.* This is the period of the great choice. It is a society glorifying the dignity of man as a human. It brings the full realization of man as an economic unit entitled not only to compensation for his labor, but to a full life of freedom. The choice facing mankind is between finding this completeness through the ministrations of the almighty State (or so promises their propaganda) or earning it in a revitalized Western-Democracy type society which is trying to correct the abuses of Period II. And from this dichotomy in the world today comes the challenge to us in a free society: can we adjust our management principles and techniques to minister to the needs of the whole man, can we dignify the worker as his eternal soul requires of us, and still out-produce and out-maneuver the socialist system?

This choice is between a system which recognizes the worker's worth as an individual, and a system which considers the worker as one more cog in a mighty machine. As Reinhard Bendix has pointed out:

> Throughout the industrialization of the West, industrial leadership has been presented as the achievement of individuals. In Russia . . . as the achievement of those who represent the nation, . . . the supreme authority of the state.[14]

And again,

> In the West . . . qualities of excellence were attributed to employers and managers which made them appear worthy of the position they occupied . . . holding out a promise to the many who with proper exertion might better themselves or even advance to positions of authority. . . . In Soviet Russia . . . the exercise of authority by the few and the subordination of the many would be justified by the service each group rendered to the achievement of goals determined for it. . . . Communism has owed its strength to the articulation of grievance against the industrial way of life. . . . All should own and plan as well as work, so that all might be free.[15]

[14] *op. cit.*, p. 10.
[15] Bendix, *op. cit.*, p. 2.

Leaving for the moment one side of the choice (i.e., those who find themselves under the "protection" of the Iron Curtain) our discussion of management theory will trace the development of this period in the West.

b. *Management theory.* During this period, the worker advanced from an unidentified human unit in an assembly line to a person of worth. In many cases, he went so far as to be able to purchase stock in the company for which he worked. He then became an owner as well as a worker; he counted; he was worth something. By the 1930's this awareness of workers as human beings was widespread. They were now thought to be co-operators, personalities, creative spirits even.

In the management literature, the "man problem" became as important as the "machine problem" and the "sales problem." Two schools developed: the "process school" which investigated the planning, organizing and controlling functions of management; and the "human relations school" which gave more attention to the people in the organization and the motivating function of management.

The Process School

In 1931, in *Onward Industry*, Mooney and Reiley gave management its first integrated theory behind an organization chart. They stressed the relationships in organization rather than mere structure. They worked out a series of sequentially arranged principles which might be summarized as follows: first is the co-ordinative principle, "an orderly arrangement of group effort, to provide unity of action in the pursuit of a common purpose." Second is the scalar principle, the grading of duties according to degree of authority and corresponding responsibility. The third is the functional principle, involving the differentiation of kinds of duties performed in the organization. Note that these principles were posited as being common to all organizations, and not especially the business enterprise.

It is this school which has led to the rash of works, still increasing, setting forth various sets of "principles," "functions," "precepts," or "guides" of management in our society today. While in the main lacking great originality, save now and then in literary form, these works are the necessary application to a given field of the present-day need to find rules of behavior all neatly bound between the covers of a textbook. And since it has taken so long for these centuries-old (some of them) principles to be divested of their shrouds, it is a good thing to get them classified and stated in terms the present-day manager, leader or aspirant can understand, to save him the arduous trial and error method of learning how to be a success.

The Human Relations School

By far the most important contribution made to management theory during this period came from the Human Relations School, led by Elton Mayo, beginning with his experiments at the Hawthorne Plant of Western Electric Company.[16] Mayo revealed that organization was more than the formal arrangement of functions so neatly categorized by Mooney and Reiley. "It is a social system, a system of cliques, grapevines, informal status systems, rituals and a mixture of logical, non-logical and illogical behavior."[17]

According to Mayo, "we are leading men, not handling robots." Therefore, higher productivity is in no way determined by positive incentives, experimental changes and working conditions. Social demands within the group resulted in the more or less tacit agreement of workers on the standards of work performance.

While Taylor believed the worker is a wage-maximizing individual in isolation, since it is his aptitude for work which counts, not his relation to fellow-workers, Mayo insisted the worker acts in natural solidarity with fellows: not responsive to appropriate incentives, but a product of personal sentiments and emotional involvements. He is non-logical thinking, with one overriding motive: desire to stand well with his fellows. Only when that fails, an emergency forces him to extricate himself by logical thinking. Mayo wanted management to reverse this, to control sentiments, develop logical thinking, conquer the "human-social facts."[18]

If all this is true, then Mayo's advice was to approach the problem from the perspective of whatever knowledge of human nature we have. He recommended the use of all social science disciplines focused on understanding and solving conflicts within the industrial system. In turn, he believed, a successful human relations approach will create

---

[16] Summarized in Scott, *op. cit.*, p. 28.
[17] Scott, *op. cit.*, p. 29.
[18] Bendix, *op. cit.*, p. 301.

organizational harmony, increased employee satisfaction and greater operational efficiency.

The Behaviorists

A further distillation of the human relations approach is that of the so-called Behaviorists who suggest we should achieve maximum results by building a framework of knowledge first, through the use of all the behavioral sciences (psychology, sociology, cultural anthropology especially, but also borrowing heavily from economics, philosophy, law, history and others). Then, by quantifying all the variables it is possible to control, we can arrive at a solution for all interpersonal conflicts in an organization.

This is the scheme presently being given widest acclaim, though many authors do not recognize their plans by the same name. But most modern approaches to the problem of greater production through greater use of the human factors of production are in reality following the behaviorist pattern. This would be true of all types of production: industrial, educative, research, political and religious service.

Professionalization of Management

In most recent years the best elements of the scientific management approach and the most successful facets of the human relations approach have crystallized into what Edward D. Jones forecast as the "professionalization of management." This had to be the result of the tremendous expansion in organization size which began with the emergence of our large corporations, bodies of government, educational institutions and service organizations of all kinds (hospitals, churches, etc.). Ownership passed from the hands of a few into the hands of the many. There are over a million stockholders in American Telephone and Telegraph Company, for instance. This contributed greatly to the professionalization trend of management and the growth of a managerial bureaucracy.

> Seen historically, bureaucratization may be interpreted as the increasing subdivision of the functions which the owners-managers of the early enterprises had performed personally. . . . As the work involved became more complex with the development of economic enterprises,

it came to be delegated to subordinates both with regard to routine work and with regard to selected aspects of the entrepreneurial function proper.[19]

For example, matters relating to hiring, firing, granting of pay increases and promotions, disciplining, hearing grievances, policy-making, etc. which formerly hinged on the decision of one man were gradually delegated to lower echelons of managers. The rights of workers were safeguarded on these matters because the final word was as a general rule not in one man's hands. Likewise, the responsibilities of managing were more carefully fulfilled because they hinged on the opinions of boards rather than sole owners.

The professional manager must be skilled in the traditional functions of management such as planning, organizing, staffing, directing and controlling. At the same time he must adequately apply the findings of the Hawthorne experiments with regard to motivating workers. Further, he must safeguard the rights of the owners of today's complicated corporate structures, for whom he acts as steward.

The Social Ethic

This, then, has been our choice in the free Western world: to entrust the responsibilities of management to a growing legion of professional managers who undertake to respect the rights of owners as well as those of workers. We do so because we believe in the brotherhood of man more than we do in the authority of the State as a prime motivator.

William G. Scott, in the work quoted earlier, speaks of the social ethic which "emphasizes the collectivity, concentrating on the interpersonal and intergroup relationships with the objective of minimizing conflict. The social ethic has grown in significance during the 20th century because of increased human interdependency and proximity."[20] Given that in this day and age there is a closer harmony among men if only because of greater proximity, we are faced with three levels of aspiration in achieving our social acceptance of others, according to Scott: the materialistic, productive-efficiency attitude; the humanistic attitude; and the theological attitude.[21]

[19] *Ibid.*, p. 211.
[20] Scott, *op. cit.*, p. 6.
[21] *Ibid.*, p. 90.

Today a management philosophy which aspires to productive efficiency and harmony in the organization cannot hope to achieve this objective after the fashion of F. W. Taylor. With Elton Mayo it must recognize human dignity. It is just a step from this proposition to the next. Human dignity is firmly rooted in the Judaeo-Christian tradition which places great weight on the worth of the individual and the brotherhood of man. Go one step further and see behind this the Mystical Body of Christ rather than the brotherhood of the proletariat, and you have chosen the theological attitude rather than the materialistic one.

Though we are yet a long way off from this epitome in the cold, calculating world of business, even in business we are heading in its direction. We do not think we have made the wrong choice in the Western world. Capitalism must in the end triumph over Communism. If it can be done by pursuing our present course, the period of the great choice will resolve itself into the period of just humanitarian management. If our present methods do not succeed in overcoming socialism, we must wage a new economic war against socialism using some yet unknown weapon.

Conclusion

The above study has attempted to trace the development of management theory by delineating a history of authority in the world from the autocracy of early times to the bureaucracy of today. We have been forced to use an analytical framework and choose as points of reference three arbitrary periods of time and their chief exponents, setting forth the underlying reason demanding in each period the emergence of its own apostle. Why did Taylor stress industrial technology? Because of the Industrial Revolution and the economic theories permitting it. Why did Mayo stress industrial sociology? Because of his era's predilection for the social sciences. Why are we today attempting to utilize all disciplines in management? Because of the modern-day emphasis on the "whole man."

Other Analytical Frameworks

Not that the historical events or economic theories we have used as a framework are the *only* underlying reasons. We said at the start of this chapter that any framework seems to be an arbitrary codification.

We might have used philosophy as a base, tracing the development of management as an expression of man's various teachings regarding the first principles. During the early centuries of the civilized world, the didacticism of Aristotle gave rise to a belief in a strong centralized type of government. This view obtained through the Middle Ages when Thomistic doctrine confirmed the authoritarian attitudes of all leaders, civil and religious. Gradually, 17th, 18th and 19th century minor lights heralded the day of revolution, perhaps beginning with Descartes' "cogito, ergo sum," a sort of declaration of independence by the individual from accepted norms and mores, and seconded by his British counterparts through Locke and Dewey who brought to the English speaking world the temerity to question the almost life-or-death rights of the lords over the laborers. And finally, of course, the modern extreme individualism of the Jean Paul Sartre type existentialists joined with Karl Marx, "champion of the proletariat" on the one hand, dividing the world against a Jacques Maritain who evokes from the teachings of his forerunners a Christian justification for recognition of the rights of the individual based on theological motives.

We might have done this, and again it would have to be said that the periods, like their underlying philosophies, are not truly successive, for each one finds in itself segments of the former, continuing to fruition as it is fertilized by new strength in the succeeding period. No period could claim the entire truth. What was good in each continued on in the next, so that the last period is built on the better elements of the former ones.

Whatever system of codification is used, it can safely be said that with the passage of time, the systematization of a body of management principles becomes ever more meaningful in what it is able to accomplish by furnishing the student of management in the school and the practicing manager in industry, in government, in the Church, with a sense of direction.

The Papal Encyclicals

Lest there be any doubt as to the direction that should be given to management theory in the opinion of this author, let us discuss one further important contribution to management literature. We believe that 100% implementation of the principles set forth in the encyclical of Pope Leo XIII, *Rerum Novarum*, would be the perfect development of a sound theory of management.

This document reduced the problem first and foremost to the recognition of the underlying eternal truths of justice and equality. Industrialists and laborers alike should begin with the simplest questions of man's purpose on earth, of the existence of human society, of the relationship between goods and services and human destiny. The primary objective of the manager and the managed must be the "sustaining and progressive perfecting" of the family of every man who works for a living. This ideal is impossible while any living person is considered less important than some inanimate material object of wealth or possession, and the end of industrial pursuit is a systematized method for amassing personal power and profit. Once these basic questions are faced up to, the collective effort of labor and management would be a decent livelihood for self and family of each human engaged in the enterprise no matter on which side. Considerations of increased dividends to owners or wages and salaries to workers would come after, and not before, this primary goal is achieved.

All the modern Popes and the recently completed Vatican Council have pursued this line of reasoning when discussing the rights of workers and owners alike. They begin with the unassailable truth that the goods of earth are for all men, that a bountiful Almighty in His providence filled the earth with His bounty to aid man in his worldly journey to an eternal destiny. Nature's materials in their raw form or transformed to a higher use by human ingenuity are meant as an aid to man in living a worthy life as a child of God. Any form of society, any interpretation of authority, any cooperative endeavor of men that deprives even one human being (to say nothing of millions) of his God-given right to the use of this wealth of nature is immoral, cruel, unjust and contrary to the fundamental purposes of creation.

This is the approach from the vantage point of social justice, which is not to say that it is mere theoretical moralizing with no roots in the earth of reality. This approach is concrete. True, it does not provide a ready answer that fixes the scale of wages or the distribution of dividends—these are details that must still be worked out by labor and management and economic advisers. But details need a foundation; the foundation should be these principles of social justice. Following these principles, all factors of industry (management, labor, the people represented by government) cooperate toward the greatest possible return to each from their united effort.

Like the Gospel whose principles are its foundation, this plan is "a hard saying." It is radical as it challenges capital's rights to unlimited profit and labor's rights to unscrupulous tactics of resistance. But it is entirely practical because it takes into consideration the most fundamental dictates of human life and human living. The chances of its acceptance universally are meager, but this author, for one, endorses it as the most constructive contribution in the entire history of management theory.

CHAPTER THREE

IMPROVING THE USE OF TIME

Universality of the Problem

One of the sure signs that a person has attained a position of some importance is the growth of demands on his time. Positions of responsibility in all walks of life seem to mean automatically increased difficulty in finding sufficient time for the accomplishment of duties. A complaint that will be recognized in later times as special to our era is the oft heard "where does the time go? There just aren't enough hours in the day!" It seems the faster our pace of life, the more things we find undone.

Priests are no exception to this general rule for managers. Nor are individual priests who have uttered this same complaint *de profundis* to feel they are unique in their profession. One impelling reason for the acceptance of the new collaboration of the laity by many priests is their earlier recognition that something had to be done to help solve this problem of finding more time.

It may be expressed in the familiar terms of the dichotomy between spiritual and temporal responsibilities, as for instance in this quotation from a busy modern parish priest:

> Reduced to the final analysis it would seem that the present-day American pastor is trying to solve the riddle of the harmonious blending of the essential elements of his priestly work with the constantly recurring and often times humanly annoying material problems. Just what the exact balance is and how to strike it would, in my estimation, be a most fundamental problem of present-day American parochial life.

Or it may be the self-criticism of honest priests who fear they are not getting everything possible out of the time spent on any of their duties because of a lack of meaningful criteria for the measurement of their performance. Witness this remark of another busy priest:

> Nowhere but in the priesthood is incompetency so well rewarded. To be a failure in the priesthood demands effort, for sins of omission don't count; in a word there is no hierarchy of authority to insure efficiency. If a time study were conducted of priests such as is done for people in business, it would be found that we are operating at about ½ of our potential.

These quotations come from a survey conducted by this author in a fourteen-state area. In this survey 846 priests out of 1453 respondents indicated they felt they did not have enough time for their primary functions of "spiritual administrations" because of the demands of temporal duties. If the full truth were known, chances are all of them could have identified this as a problem, even though not all felt they were having difficulty in coping with it.

This is why Peter Drucker gives as the first of his five practices—or habits—of an effective manager, the ability to know where his time goes. It should be noted that these words are carefully chosen. He does not say "the ability to control all of his time," but "to know where his time goes." So the effective priest-manager may not control much more of his time than an ineffective priest-manager (perhaps because other people are controlling it for him) but he is aware of this fact and plans his own work and that of others accordingly.

A program for improving the use of one's time might well include four major topics:

1. Analysis of present use of time.
2. Questioning each present expenditure of time.
3. Development of improved schedule.
4. Developing better management methods.

Suggested Method for Analyzing Present Use of Time

The first step in improving the use of one's time is to analyze how it is presently being used. This process may follow three simple steps.

Step One. Ask yourself what you are now doing. List all the current expenditures of your time as in a diary. This means literally to sit down at the end of a day and review the way you have spent your time in the past twenty-four hours. Record each major block of time and how you spent it. Do not try to account for every segment of two or three minutes or you will soon go out of your mind. Rather, learn to think in chunks of time; that is, account for every hour, every half-hour, maybe even every fifteen minutes.

To do this faithfully requires the same kind of patience, honesty and self-searching that is required to keep an accurate diary, or closer to home, to do a thorough job in the particular examination of conscience which is a part of the daily routine of many priests.

You must do this for a whole week, or better, for a month in order to get a rather complete picture of the kinds of things on which you are spending your time. If you have a secretary, you might enlist her aid in helping you maintain this diary at least for the normal business hours when she is around.

Step Two. Classify the time expenditures which you have recorded. You will probably find that all the things you have been spending your time doing can conveniently be grouped into three natural categories as follows:

a) Regular or recurring duties—the routine operations which keep the wheels turning. You might say these are the bread and butter operations of the organization you are administering. Examples of such time expenditures would be: opening and answering routine correspondence, paying bills, answering telephone calls for routine information, eating three square meals a day, saying Mass and administering the sacraments, etc. It is important to notice that *routine* does not necessarily mean *unimportant*. Certainly officiating in liturgical ceremonies is not unimportant. *Routine* here means *repetitive* or *recurring*.

b) Emergencies, or problems which you solve. These time expenditures have to do with putting out the brush fires that seem to spring up all over the place. Certainly a large portion of a typical priest-manager's time is involved in reconciling divergent opinions, settling squabbles, granting permissions for projects that have not been pursued on a routine basis, answering public charges, rushing to the chancery office to explain the financial position or a report and the like. In general, this kind of time expenditure can not be detected because of its unplanned nature. These are as a rule the crisis situations which come upon us either because we did not plan for them in advance, or because we had no way of knowing they would arise.

c) Developmental or innovative duties. These are the things we do of a creative nature because of their significance for long-term improvement of the regular operations or to prevent recurrence of crisis situations. As a rule also, this is the kind of thing that we usually do not spend enough time on. It is the research and development portion of our day which often is overlooked completely.

Step Three. Ask yourself what else you should be doing, especially in view of the results you are now getting given the present way you spend your time. A look at Figure 3 may help to explain this step. The figure assumes that your diary of time expenditures has indicated that approximately 60% of your time is spent on routine duties, 35% on crises, and 5% on innovations. This, of course, accounts for 100% of the time you are now spending on your various duties. The assumption is that, like most people, you often feel that there are other things that are not getting done, results that are not being achieved, because you just don't have the time for them. You should then add a list of other things that you feel you should have the time to do. Figure 3 calls these "additional time expenditures" which might, for example, total another 20% of your daily time for a new grand total of 120%. Obviously you only have 100% of your time available for all duties, so the problem is to adjust your present use of time so as to make room for the 20% additional. In the practical order this means squeezing 20% of the water out of your present time expenditures to make room for the additional 20%. This, in turn, means questioning each of your present time expenditures and takes us to the next major question.

```
Present Time Expenditures

        Routine        60% ⎫
        Crises         35% ⎬  20% of the water
        Innovatives     5% ⎭  to be squeezed out
        Total         100%

Additional Time

        Expenditures    20%
        Grand Total
```

FIGURE 3

Question Each Present Expenditure of Time

If you are to make room for the additional duties you would like to perform, you must examine your present time expenditures seeking those which could be eliminated, modified, combined, or perhaps delegated to someone else. Hence, it is necessary to question seriously each duty you now perform as indicated in your diary by posing questions such as:

a) Why is it necessary?
b) What is its essential purpose?
c) When should it be done? What is its priority?
d) Who should do it?
e) Where should it be done?
f) How should it be done?

What you are doing by subjecting each expenditure of time to these questions is sorting out the things which you not only *are* doing but *should* be doing.

The principle recommended to be followed here is the principle of subsidiarity. This means, of course, that a person should reserve to himself only those things which others in the administrative organization cannot do. There are certain things which require the training, the professional experience, the perspective or vantage point of your particular position in the organizational hierarchy, etc., and which therefore cannot be handled satisfactorily by anyone except yourself. These are the things you should be doing. Others you should attempt to delegate to someone else.

You will find both kinds (those you should retain and those you would like to delegate) among the routine duties, the crises, and the innovative time expenditures as well. So then the idea is not necessarily to eliminate all regular or recurring duties as if these are automatically the ones to be purged; we have mentioned, for example, liturgical functions which require the ordained status and therefore must be retained by the priest even though they are routine or repetitive.

At this point, it should be remembered, we are merely identifying time expenditures which you would *like* to transfer, modify, eliminate, or delegate as the case might be. This does not necessarily mean you can do so. Whether or not you can will depend on your own ability to develop an improved schedule of personal time expenditure as well as on the availability of others to assist in carrying out some of the things you are now doing.

Development of an Improved Schedule

Discussion with administrators in various walks of life have pointed to some of the following as ways of squeezing the water out of your present daily schedule. The list is offered as a series of thought starters which the priest-manager who is anxious to improve the use of his management time must apply to his own particular daily duties.

1. Planning so that the important things are accomplished while the less essential matters wait. (A recommended procedure for doing this will be outlined in detail in the next subsection).

2. Delegating where possible so that things can be done without you yourself doing them. (The entire next chapter will be devoted to a detailed discussion of delegation).

3. Investing in training of subordinates so that they will be more self-sufficient in their own responsibilities and in taking on some additional work from you with more confidence.

4. Keeping meetings and conversations on the beam so that they can accomplish what they are expected to accomplish with a minimum expenditure of time.

5. Controlling telephone time either by more precise screening of incoming calls, by doing less "visiting" on the phone or by avoiding overinitiation of telephone communications yourself.

6. Reducing direct close supervision of others. Your followers, if qualified, well trained and properly instructed will get more done without anyone breathing down their necks.

7. Eliminating unnecessary writing, reading, talking. The key word here is "unnecessary." This is a skill which must be developed like other communications skills.

8. Increasing your reading speed and still retaining comprehension. A large part of your job involves reading and it has been found that reading speed can be increased by as much as several hundred percent in many cases.

9. Improving records management, files, etc., so that information can be found promptly.

10. Differentiating the kinds of decisions to be made. Decisions on relatively minor matters probably should not be reaching you at all; but if they do they often will not warrant using as much time or energy as the more important decisions.

11. Taking good notes in conferences, meetings, etc. and using them well.

12. Utilizing a secretary, receptionist, bookkeeper, etc. as the need might be; or using your present assistants (clerical and lay) more effectively.

13. Relaxing now and then. Working under excess pressure leads to diminishing returns and gets others upset. Take a breather and then pick up again when you are refreshed.

14. Challenging every job, every report, every meeting—why is this necessary? Who else can do it or should be there? What will it accomplish? Can it be reduced or possibly eliminated.

15. Giving instructions in writing wherever possible. This will often reduce misunderstanding and the need for time for repeated verbal orders.

16. "Doing it now" whenever possible. "Doing it later" may often mean rereading, failing to reach the people you need to reach, interruption by other matters, etc. Where the energy, time, and probably efficiency is best at the time, consider "doing it now."

17. Determining whether telephoning, writing, or visiting would produce the best results in communication in the least time. Which one? On what occasions?

18. Working on certain problems during your best and most productive hours. For some individuals the morning hours are best; for others the afternoon or evening. This factor varies with habit, time with least interruptions, periods of best concentration, etc.

Developing Even Better Managerial Methods for Yourself

Even after you have delegated as many duties as possible according to the principle of subsidiarity, there will always remain the problem of spending a most efficient amount of time on those duties which do require your own personal attention. This, in turn, means that you must constantly seek to improve your methods of management in such areas as:

a) Developing plans.
b) Establishing objectives and standards.
c) Developing people.
d) Making decisions.
e) Communicating (interviews and discussions, writing, reading, meetings, telephone time, travel).
f) Relationships with others.
g) Reviewing and measuring results.

One specific technique that has been found helpful by many executives for the expenditure of their time has to do with the establishment of an order of priority on things to be accomplished.

The idea here is to set aside a few moments at the beginning or end of each day in order to establish a list of the things you absolutely want to get done in the course of the coming work day. This can be done by using a desk calendar appointment book or by simply taking out the back of a used envelope and noting the five or six (or eighteen or nineteen) things that you want to accomplish. Then reviewing the entire list you will assign a number to each item on the list according to your personal evaluation of its priority. When you are through you will have a list of items each with a number telling you in what order the job should be taken care of.

When you start your day's work you begin on item number one and continue working on it until it is completed. The concept of a *completed task* is the important one here. You should not move from the first item to item number two until you have completed it or at least have done all that you possibly can on it pending additional information or assistance from someone else. This is to fight against the rather common bad habit of constantly jumping from one job to another so that we always have a number of half-finished jobs in the works but never seem to get any single thing completely accomplished. The emphasis on all our management duties is to be on results, that is, accomplished tasks.

Having completed item number one, you are ready to begin item number two, and so on through your list. Should you find that because of interruptions, crises, unforeseen difficulties in completing early items on the list, etc., you don't get beyond, say, the first three items on your list, this should not cause you any dismay. Even though you had intended to complete six or seven (or eighteen or nineteen) items, and yet only got three of them done, at least you know that *by your own* determination and priorities you have done the three most important items on your list and they are now done. The remaining items on your list are merely carried over to the next day and even though in the short run you have not done as much as you would have liked to, in the long run this procedure will eventually mean a greater number of jobs totally accomplished because of the self-discipline of working at one duty at a time until it is completed and in the proper order of priority.

At this point one might ask skeptically: "Planning your day's activities that way sounds great, but who can plan when so many unforeseeable things come up?"

This is a valid question. One would have to be naïve to think that today's busy priest-manager, given the many responsibilities he has, could plan ahead the way he will spend each of his blocks of time in the course of his working day. But that is not the point. Even though much of our time is controlled by others, as was mentioned at the beginning of this chapter, the question is: do we know how much of our time is controlled by others and whether we control the time that remains?

When corporation executives such as the Chairman of the Board of General Motors Corporation have disciplined themselves to the diary procedure outlined in this chapter, they have frequently found that fully 75% of their time might be beyond their own power to control. That is to say ¾ of their time was spent answering crises, solving problems, bailing subordinates out of difficulty, etc., rather than carrying out their carefully planned schedule for their own personal duties. What surprised them was that it was only 75% of their time and not 100%. Because of the great amount of time they knew they were spending on such activities, they often tended to assume that it was impossible to control any of their time at all. They learned through this method that despite the frequent interruptions and demands on their time, there was still some percentage of time, even if only 25%, which they could control, and which they therefore should plan for, rather than allow this final 25% to slip through their fingers along with the rest.

Summary

The matter of improving the use of one's time boils down to a frank appraisal of the present expenditure of time and the creative approach to finding new ways of doing old jobs by the use of available resources. To do this one asks himself:

1. What interferes with the effective use of my management time?
2. What can I do to minimize these interferences?
3. What are the high priority demands on my time?
4. What should be considered in establishing priority?
5. On which management functions should I be spending more time and how am I going to get this time?

CHAPTER FOUR

THE ART OF DELEGATION

It was suggested in the preceding chapter that one of the most important ways to improve the use of your time is to delegate to others some of the things you are now doing. This, of course, is often much easier to say than to do. Effective delegation is a real art accomplished with grace and finesse by those who have a true understanding and appreciation of its fine points, but butchered by those who do not respect its principles.

A Mundane Example

Not too long ago a cousin of mine who lives in the suburbs found himself on a Saturday afternoon with the unpleasant task of removing the mess left by a water works crew who had recently laid a new drainage pipe across the front of his property. After burying the pipe they left an 18-inch mound of sand and stones, running along 75 feet of his property frontage. My cousin had intended to take in a ball game that afternoon but got out the tractor and cart and began the tedious job of loading the dirt and carrying it to the pond which adjoined his property.

He hadn't had time to make even one trip, however, when his good friend and neighbor from across the road came over and began to tell him of his own troubles, especially with the poor soil mixture over on that side of the road. The neighbor had no sooner finished telling how his soil was so hard that water just ran off it, when he noticed my cousin's mound of sand and stones. "Say Bill," he said, "what I really need is some sandy dirt like you've got here. You wouldn't care to let me have some of this now would you?"

"Well, I don't know," said my cousin. "I was just about to move it myself."

"Aw, come on Bill. I sure could use it. And since you've got the tractor all hitched up here, how about letting me use it so I can take this dirt over to my place?"

After an appropriate interval my cousin allowed himself to be talked into going to the ball game while the neighbor eagerly did his sand removal job for him.

Speaking of the incident later, my cousin allowed as how he had pulled "a Tom Sawyer" on his friend. You will recall how Tom was charged with whitewashing his aunt's fence when he had planned all sorts of fun for the day. Failing in his first attempt to enlist aid by too direct an approach he then resorted to what management consultant Nathaniel Stewart calls the Tom Sawyer theory of delegation.

Ben Rogers hove in sight presently—the very boy, of all boys, whose ridicule he had been dreading. Ben's gait was a hop—skip—jump—proof enough that his heart was light and his anticipations high.

Tom went on whitewashing paying no attention. Ben stared a moment and then said:

'Hi yi, yer a skunk ain't ya.'

No answer. Tom surveyed his last touch with the eye of an artist and then gave his brush another sweep and surveyed the results as before. Tom's mouth watered for Ben's apple, but he stuck to his work. Ben said:

'Hello ole chap, you gotta work eh?'

Tom wheeled suddenly and said:

'Why it's you Ben, I warn't noticin'.'

'I'm goin swimmin I am, don't ya wish ya could, but of course ya'd druther work—wouldn't ya? Course ya would!'

Tom contemplated the boy a bit and said:

'Whadda ya call work?'

'Why, ain't that work?'

Tom resumed his whitewashing and answered carelessly:

'Well maybe it is and maybe it ain't, all I know is that it suits Tom Sawyer. Does a boy get a chance to whitewash a fence everyday?'

That put the thing in a new light. Presently, Ben said:

'Say Tom, let me whitewash a little!'

Tom considered, was about to consent, but he altered his mind:

'No, no, I reckon it wouldn't hardly do Ben, ya see Aunt Polly's awful perticuler about this fence—right here on the street ya know—

if it was the back fence I wouldn't mind and she wouldn't either. Yes, she's awful perticuler about this fence; it's got to be done very careful; I reckon there ain't one boy in a thousand, maybe two thousand, that could do it the way it's got to be done.'

'Oh, is that so. Oh come now, let me just try, only just a little. I'd let ya if ya were me Tom. I'll give ya the core of my apple.'

'Well here; no Ben, now don't, I'm afraid.'

'I'll give you all of it.'

Tom gave up the brush with reluctance on his face but alacrity in his heart and while Ben worked and sweated in the sun, the retired artist sat on a barrel in the shade close by dangling his legs, munched his apple, and planned the slaughter of more innocents.

—Mark Twain, *The Adventures of Tom Sawyer*, Ch. 2.

Some Fundamentals Involved

The need for delegation does not begin with an organization chart or formal administrative structure. It begins with a priest who is so tied to his desk that he doesn't have time to take part in the community activities or services for his people which he feels are more in keeping with his role as explained in the Vatican II documents. The secret of success is not in doing your own work but in recognizing the right man to do it. Delegation has to be carefully planned to fit what the subordinate thinks is proper (though not the way Tom Sawyer did it, obviously).

When we delegate we are asking others to share something that we have. Often there is a misunderstanding of what it is that we are sharing. We frequently hear it said that when we delegate to others, we are asking them to share our responsibilities. If by *responsibilities*, we mean *duties*, then it is true that we are asking others to share in our responsibilities. The trouble comes from the fact that *responsibility* in an administrative sense more appropriately refers to our *accountability*. Many people who delegate act as though they are divesting themselves of their responsibilities—meaning accountability —when they delegate to others. How often have we inquired of someone as to the status of a particular project, only to be told, "Oh, I thought so and so took care of that. I turned the whole thing over to him"—as if the delegation of the duty to the third party could absolve us from the responsibility of having to account for the actions of the third party. I submit that this is often the case because of the misuse of the word "responsibility."

The illustration from Tom Sawyer ought to make it clear that what Tom was sharing with Ben Rogers was hardly the *duty* of white-washing the fence, but the job and *privilege* of being allowed to whitewash the fence. And in this regard what we really share when we delegate to others is our *power*, our ability to make decisions in the area covered by the *duties* that we have been assigned. The proper sequence of what takes place in delegation, then, seems to be the following:

1. We recognize that we need assistance in handling all of our responsibilities.
2. We invite someone to share in the work by assigning to them a portion of our *duties*.
3. We give to them the necessary *power* to carry out the duties that have just been assigned to them.
4. We create in them a new accountability for the work that we have assigned to them which corresponds to the accountability we have to our own administrative superiors.

Formal vs. Earned Authority

Many clergymen shy away from the concept of delegation out of a mistaken idea that delegation is one of the trappings of a decadent system of authority which is the butt of almost universal attack in society today. I say mistaken notion because the concept of authority here held differs from the strawman which is the subject of attack today.

One does not have to have a position of superiority in order to delegate. As a matter of fact, he who relies upon his positional authority (i.e., that deriving from his formal position in the administrative structure) always has found it next to impossible to get the cooperation of his subordinates. There is a much different and more effective aspect of authority, called "earned authority," which can be defined as "the position of excellence or respect which one enjoys in the company of others because of some quality in himself commanding this respect rather than because of position or title alone."

Tom Sawyer would probably have wound up painting the fence himself had he endeavored to command Ben Rogers to assist him in the whitewashing. But by shrewd estimation of what it would take to earn the cooperation of his young playmate he was soon able to achieve the degree of cooperation he desired.

Authority in the Post-Vatican Era

In the mind of many the "Soaring Sixties" are really more aptly called the "Rebellious Sixties." It seems that in all walks of life people are rebelling against constituted authority. Employees strike to make known their demands; students in our colleges (and high schools) demonstrate against the school administration; self-righteous citizens rebel against decisions made in the political and military spheres. Indignant parishioners even register disagreement with pastoral assignments or decisions to close a parish. In every sphere of life people are not only questioning but openly opposing decisions made by those in authority.

Does this mean we will soon see the overthrow of all lawful authority? Will the 70's be marked by anarchy? Will the unrest against those in positions of power end only when all authority and the order that comes with authority are replaced by a freedom that knows no constraint?

There are probably some rebels who hope so. But the majority of those who are uneasy under the reins of today's leaders are not really opposed to the concept of order or organization or the necessity to have someone in a position of leadership.

What does motivate them is an innate desire to play some role in arriving at the decision in question, be it in the economic, diplomatic or religious sphere. Psychologists tell us this is the nature of man—he wishes to have a say in the decisions that affect him. The man on the assembly line wants to have a say in how fast his machine will operate; the student wants to have a say in what courses will be offered; the young men who fight our wars want to have a say in what world-wide commitments our nation makes. In a word, they are against (or in favor of) not authority itself, or the person in authority, but the decision made by that person.

Without launching into the theology of the role of the Church in the modern world (a subject far beyond the competence of this author), it is becoming more and more clear that authority in the Church today should not be looked upon as identical to authority as mistakenly viewed by its opponents: i.e., an ordering of those who rule and those who are ruled. Since the Church is a community gathered to live the life of Christ, authority in it means a ministry to be performed in the service of the community. In this regard authority, like administration as a whole, means the exercise of leadership. It means the responsibility for keeping the members of the community united; keeping them directed toward their common goals; and controlling their activities protectively so that their goals may be achieved. (Attention is invited to the definition of leadership in Chapter One.)

It is not surprising to find the same desire to share in making parish decisions in all those whose lives will be affected: priests, religious and laity. Yet before the Second Vatican Council, it was the rare parish wherein there was any opportunity to do so. The typical parish has been highly monarchical in accordance with earlier concepts of Church government patterned after a "function-oriented community" as discussed in previous sections. All authority was vested in the pastor, and this highly centralized authority was rarely shared with others to any great extent. Sometimes this was due to the pastor's fear of "letting things get out of hand." Sometimes it was rather the case of his not knowing how to release some of his authority and responsibilities while retaining the control he felt he must maintain as the sole person accountable to the Ordinary for what happens in the parish.

Collegiality, the term used to describe the relationship between the Pope and the entire body of bishops, is often extended to describe the relationships between the pastor and his people. Some interpret collegiality as being synonymous with democracy, i.e., that the will of the people is supreme and all power comes from the people and is passed upward to those in authority. It is difficult to reconcile this with the fact that the threefold authority to teach, to govern, and to sanctify was given by Christ directly to St. Peter and the Apostles and to their successors.

How does this distinction manifest itself in the parish? In some parishes where attempts are being made by the pastor to share the burdens of administration with advisory "boards," the complaint is often heard that the board members are "only" advisory, as if the giving of advice and the furnishing of information and arguments pro and con were not part of the decision-making process.

Actually, the arrival at a decision is only the last step in a series. The preliminaries to that step must include gathering of facts, examining the implications of these facts, determining what other people think of the facts, weighing various alternatives, analyzing the consequences of possible action. Then there comes the point where deliberation stops and the decision must be made. And whether the decision is made by a vote of a policy-making board, or by the single vote of a pastor after listening to his advisory board, the preliminaries play a vital role in making the decision.

The Exercise of Authority

Whatever form the structure of authority in the parish takes, how it is exercised is where the family spirit of Vatican II will come into play. Just as in our individual homes, father differs from father in the way in which he secures the obedience of his children, so in the parish family, all those sharing positions of authority must choose a way to use their authority. In the past this authority was often exercised autocratically, almost in military fashion. A kind of blind obedience was required in the name of discipline. Priests built monuments to their own name and scolded the people into paying for them. Lay persons in parish organizations used their positions to win friends and influence people or to further private business ventures.

This was reliance on what we have already referred to as *positional* authority whereby a man relied on his position to get people to follow his directions. Today, in various walks of life, the emphasis is on *earned* authority whereby a man works at getting people to follow him by showing them he *deserves* to be listened to.

Even in the military of the 20th century, success depends less on iron discipline than on the resourcefulness of small groups working together as a team, whether it be a combat squad, a missile launching team or the general staff at headquarters. Each member relies as much on the technical abilities and level of performance of others as on the formal authority structure.

In industry today also, research has proven that effectiveness can be achieved only when as much discretion and independence as possible is left to subordinates. The criterion of success is the ability to obtain consent, to promote effective participation, rather than compliance out of deference.

So, too, in the parish what is desired is a manner of exercising authority which enlists the consent of all, not as unthinking automatons, but as rationally participating and contributing members. There is more to authority than giving orders. It includes seeking the insights and knowledge and skills of others and promoting the fullest possible participation of all who are affected.

But this extended meaning of collegiality is not synonymous with democracy. The will of the people is not supreme; all power does not come from the people, being passed upward to those with authority. St. Paul expressed the direction authority takes quite differently: "Let everyone be subject to the higher authorities for there exists no authority except from God, and those who exist have been appointed by God" (Rom 13:1).

Commenting on the discussions of authority taking place since Vatican II, Pope Paul VI stressed that "the representatives of Christ have pastoral authority and are given the charisms of magisterium . . . for the service and salvation of the people of God . . . the Church is hierarchical not amorphous. It is not democratic in a sense that no one has priority in matters of faith and doctrines over the one whom the Holy Spirit has placed as the head of the Church of God. This means in other words that the Lord has entrusted to some of its members the task of giving to their fellow members the services of authority and of direction as a principle of unity, or order, and of solidarity in effective working together."[1]

Freedom and Authority

Still, in exercising authority those in positions of responsibility should begin with the God-given idea of freedom which all baptized persons have, always respecting this freedom and limiting it only if necessary for the common good. In this manner, authority will become control—or law—and will be able to coordinate activities of functions and not people.

There are some who believe that the Church shares many of the characteristics of other large organizations. It has vast numbers of people, manifold intermediate objectives all connected with its ultimate goal, a complex system of communications, etc. Because this

[1] Address on Candlemas Day 1967, to clergy of Rome and representatives of religious orders.

is so, because the Church is composed of human beings associating together to achieve a common end, some believe we can learn much about the exercise of authority by examining how it is done in other human organizations. For example, priest-sociologist, Fr. Joseph Fichter, points out five principles of social science research which "although obvious . . . do not seem to be practiced by bishops and clergy in the Catholic Church":

1. Human beings must be treated as responsible persons. This is not done when the bishop lacks trust in his priests or the pastors do not trust the parishioners.
2. The person expected to perform must be in a position "where he is able to perform." He should not be expected to do only what he is told to do, and he should be picked for his job only on the basis that he is competent, wants to do the job and has been given the authority to do it.
3. Recognition and appreciation must be given to people in recognition of what they do.
4. People must be advised of how their work is rated and how they themselves are being evaluated.
5. There should be open communications and information about prospective changes and programs so that any element of surprise is reduced.

Adherence to these principles makes it possible for persons in authority to exercise their functions of unity, direction and correction, and at the same time allow followers to enjoy freedom in carrying out their responsibilities. It results in an exercise of authority and a practice of obedience which promotes intelligent cooperation between superiors and those subject to authority. As far as possible, the suggestions of the leader should be so explained that those who receive them can understand, accept and participate effectively in the purpose of the work.

Far from being treated like a robot or a child, the person is made to feel a sense of responsibility and allowed to exercise his judgment. Usually, the leader will specify the results he expects, and leave the choice of means and techniques to the one whose responsibility it is to perform the task. In this way, the freedom and self-respect of the one subject to authority are preserved and he is allowed to work, grow and develop with the freedom of the People of God.

The Practice of Delegation

What is real delegation?

Activities within the normal range of a follower's duties only? No! Those duties more appropriately make up his job as distinct from yours.

Work leading up to the identification of a problem, but with the decision-making prerogative reserved to yourself? No! This is drudgery, not a sharing in your authority.

Working on a problem, but subject to the review and analysis of a decision-making group, even a parish council? No! In that case the council or group would be sharing your authority but not the person doing the work.

"Farming out" of a part of your job and problems together with full responsibility to handle it and make a decision? Yes!

Explaining the *what* and *why* of a special problem to a follower, but leaving the *how* of the task of solving it up to his judgment? Yes again!

Remembering a few fundamental principles as essentials in the delegation process will remove most of the mystery of this critical management skill. Among the most important elements are:

1. The follower must have a "feel" for the total situation he is being asked to help out in.
2. He must have a clear understanding of existing policies, systems, constraints within which he must do his work.
3. The goal, time, volume and similar specifics of the end product required must be clarified.
4. There must be an understanding of what is expected in terms of the yardsticks to be used in measuring satisfactory performance of the delegated task.
5. There must be free communications available between the follower and yourself, within reasonable bounds.
6. He must be given sufficient authority to handle the task assigned, with others who might be involved made aware of this authority.
7. There should be agreement on a check list of control points, interim reports if necessary, or tentative "get-togethers" agreed upon to keep you at all times informed of progress on the task.

8. All this assumes the follower is prepared by a combination of native ability, experience and/or training to handle the assignment.

9. Don't rush in and take over in the middle of the project (barring calamitous results, of course). Often the job won't go as well as it might if you were doing it: but this is how followers are trained to be worth more to you.

10. Don't expect perfection. Again, it takes training and experience to become adept at the work. Early impatience from you will do more to keep followers from even wanting to help you in your work than any other thing.

11. Finally, in assigning work, do not pass on a job that you are finding too difficult for yourself to handle. Work that requires special talents you don't have—e.g., training in accounting or curriculum preparation, etc.—is one thing, and you may be expected to seek help from others in these jobs as a matter of getting trained assistance. But "hot potatoes" decisions affecting the whole parish, for example, which you are afraid of making yourself because of possible "flak" from the people, are poor assignments to delegate, because then it's merely "passing the buck," and the leader does not become relieved of the responsibility just because he delegates the decision!

Why We Don't Delegate

Professor Earl Brooks (Cornell Graduate School of Business and Public Administration)[2] in a national survey of executives found the reasons most often given for not delegating:

1. The most common excuse for not delegating is that the *subordinates have less experience* than the chief. They are too new or too young.

    But as one executive put it: "Swimming can't be learned without getting into the water."

2. Impatient executives defend their do-it-yourself practices by observing that explaining delegation *takes more time than it's worth.*

    At first this may be true. But the only way a subordinate

---

[2] "Get More Done—Easier," *Nation's Business,* Oct. 1962.

can develop ability to take on bigger assignments is through systematic training and coaching.

3. Many executives feel they *can't risk a mistake.*

   With adequate controls most mistakes can be avoided. We spend considerable time checking before we approve a project. We spend time in review and investigations after the action, particularly if results are unsatisfactory. But seldom is enough time spent checking as delegated responsibilities are being performed.

4. Several managers were reluctant to delegate because they felt that *their rank got them quicker action* than a subordinate could get.

   If you have to devote extra time to get rapid action, you may be neglecting your other functions.

5. "I am *solely responsible*. How can I delegate?" ask the more cautious managers.

   Although the chief is responsible ultimately for the actions and decisions of all his subordinates, a limited number of decisions must be made by designated subordinates. The chief can meet his responsibility through understood assignments and authority, controls, measures of performance, and systems of accountability rather than by personally doing a multitude of tasks.

6. "My subordinates are *specialists*. They lack interest in overall management problems and do not have ready access to information needed for certain decisions," is a reason frequently given by managers in charge of technically or scientifically trained subordinates.

   The general rule for eating an elephant—cut it up in pieces—may apply here with delegation of specified areas for action and possible use of task forces which could combine a group of several special skills.

7. "My people are *already too busy*," is a common observation.

   Probably they are, but what are they doing that could be eliminated, modified, or delegated so that they could be of even more help to you?

   An overly occupied manager who was signing sheafs of papers which had already been signed by three other subordinates was asked: "Do you know what you are signing?"

Creating the Proper Environment

As suggested by Figure 4, the goal in becoming a good delegator is to provide the environment which will encourage people to develop

```
DELEGATION

THE GOAL IS TO PROVIDE THE ENVIRONMENT
WHICH WILL ENCOURAGE PEOPLE TO DEVELOP
THEMSELVES  -  BECOME SELF-RESPONSIBLE

Which do your people do when a problem comes up?


1.  Ignore the problem?


2.  Take the problem to you?


3.  Take it to you with alternatives?


4.  Take your alternatives and a recommendation?


5.  Solve the problem and tell you about it later?
```

FIGURE 4

themselves, to become self-responsible. Most of the reasons why delegation fails are linked to the failure on the part of the leader to provide this kind of environment. You can test this out on yourself by applying the question of Figure 4 to your own situation and your own people.

SITUATION ONE:

Assume you are a pastor in a parish, or the administrator of an institution. You have a custodial force with a head maintenance man in charge of upkeep, repairs, etc. Early one morning this follower of yours comes upon a broken window in one of the staircases in the building.

The question is: What is this man likely to do?

Figure 4 presents five possible alternatives.

1. He could ignore the problem. Seeing the broken window, recognizing it should be fixed, but also knowing that you always tell him what to do about such things, he could adopt a "wait until I'm told what to do about it" attitude. This might be his reaction, for example, if every time he had tried to use a little initiative, he'd been told quite clearly that he is being paid to do what he is told—period.

2. He could bring the problem to you—tell you about the broken window, in case you had not noticed it, and then ask what you want him to do about it. Here, he is being a little more helpful than putting his head in the sand and hoping for the problem to take care of itself, but for all practical purposes, he still is dumping it in your lap.

3. He could bring the problem to you and mention several alternatives. He could mention that he has a supply of glass on hand and he just happens to have the time himself to replace the broken window pane; or he could suggest that one of the boys around the building might enjoy picking up a little pocket money after school hours replacing the pane; or you could consider calling the hardware store down the street and have them come out to fix the window since no one else had the time; etc.

Here he has done some thinking about the problem, and is making you aware of various ways of solving it, but again he is relying on you to make the decision.

4. He could bring you the problem, mention some alternatives and recommend a solution. Here he analyzes the pro's and con's of each of the alternatives he mentions, and makes an outright recommendation for solving the problem.

This is obviously of much more help to you, because it saves you the time of checking out the relative advantages of each of the alternatives, and requires only your approval of the completed plan. (This approach is often referred to as "completed staff work," which is a concept implying that good delegates should assist you in such a way that they present you with a completed package ready for your approval, and supported with all the necessary answers to any question you might logically be expected to have.)

5. He could solve the problem, if it is within the scope of his authority, and report to you about it later on.

This is manifestly more helpful to you than any other possibility. But it requires that he and you have a clear understanding as to what the limits of his authority are. You would probably not want him replacing a $15,000 heating plant, and then telling you about it later on.

Furthermore, it also requires that a report be made about what he has done in keeping with the scope of his authority, so that you at least know that the problem arose, and that it was duly taken care of.

SITUATION TWO:

You are a pastor. You have a co-pastor who is responsible for getting out the parish bulletin. Your only restriction on Father in carrying out this assigned responsibility is that he must get it printed or put out each week at a reasonable cost. That's the only limitation you've given him.

Now, for some months he's been using a certain secretary right there in the rectory to do this, on a mimeograph machine, and it came out a rather low-cost and reasonably presentable kind of a bulletin. One fine day the secretary tells you, the pastor, that she cannot continue to do this work: it's just taking too much of her time, and so you tell Father that he is going to have to find another way of getting the bulletin out because your secretary cannot do it any longer.

Once again, the question is: what is Father likely to do?

1. He could ignore the problem or hope it goes away, or wait until you give him further instructions, or say "Well, you're the cause of my not being able to use the person I had before, so you figure it out, Buster," or something like that. This would not be showing much initiative.

2. Or, Father might go one step further. He might not just sit back and ignore the problem; he might just come to you some day and say "Father, you know this problem we have in getting the bulletin out. Well, now we had this change in the secretary and you know what it's going to mean to me and my bulletin, and will you please tell me

now how I am going to get my bulletin out?" Here again, he is just bringing it to you for a solution.

3. He might go one step further. In bringing the problem to you for a solution, he might have stopped first and asked himself: are there different ways we might handle this problem, in case I am asked? So he might be ready to mention the possibility of hiring a part-time girl, or getting a school girl to do it, or taking it over to the nuns, or farming it out to one of the parish groups to get it done commercially, etc., etc. Now he's not just counting on you, but he's doing some thinking himself (and who knows, he just might come up with a good answer to a rather common problem in parish life).

4. If he goes still further, he might explore the relative costs and time and problems of all kinds that might be associated with each of his alternative solutions, and come up with a single recommended solution among the possible ones. Now he is coming to you with a recommended solution for the problem, with completed staff work.

5. Finally, if he has more initiative still, he might recognize that something has to be done, that you have entrusted him with the job with the single constraint of "reasonable cost," that you have other things to be busy about. And so he might avail himself of the alternative which he judges best and then let you know later on how he solved the problem.

The point in both of these situations is that you, as leader, create the climate which will cause the follower to act either up near the top of Figure 4, i.e., with little initiative, or near the bottom of Figure 4, i.e., as a real help to you. If you encourage people to bother you with details of their assigned work, they will believe this is expected of them, and they will develop behavior patterns accordingly. On the other hand, if you take a hard line, if you say to them firmly, "Details of that kind are your responsibility; please take care of them," then they will develop self-reliant patterns of behavior. In either case, the kind of people you have, the extent to which they accept and handle delegated tasks is more a reflection of you and your methods of leading than it is of them and their ability to be followers.

CHAPTER FIVE

STYLES OF LEADERSHIP

The first practice of an effective administrator which we have been discussing so far concerns the ability to control the use of time. We have seen in the two preceding chapters that this hinges greatly upon our ability to obtain the willing cooperation of other people in sharing our duties. Since the success we may expect to have in doing this, as well as in exercising the other skills of administration which we shall discuss in succeeding chapters, in turn depends upon the way we "deal with people," it would be helpful at this point to discuss alternative styles of leadership, that is, the various ways in which administrators do handle people.

At the risk of oversimplifying a very complex subject, we might say that a manager's particular style of leadership will depend primarily on which of the qualities of leadership he chooses to emphasize. To take a simplistic view, two paramount qualities of leadership have been identified in all the research that has been going on in recent decades concerning leader-follower relationships.

One is the element of concern for the welfare of people that work for you—not in the paternalistic sense—but in the warm genuine human sense: "I want to be able to help in any way I can to make your life on the job a more satisfactory one. I am concerned with your welfare. I am concerned to treat you fairly, to deal with you honestly."

Element #2 is what could almost be called tough supervision. It is setting high standards and demanding that people measure up to those standards. It is the competence quality of leadership.

The interesting thing that is coming out in research is that if you take either one of these factors alone you have nothing. If you have the man who is full of warm concern for his people but doesn't care how they perform, people don't have any respect for him at all. If you take the man who merely sets high standards—who is firm and

tough and demanding but doesn't have any feeling for his people—
they are sore at him. But put the two together and you've got some
of the central core of effective leadership in an industrial organization.[1]

The two basic styles of leadership which can be identified center
around which of these two elements becomes uppermost in the mind
of the leader. On the one hand there are those supervisors, leaders
and administrators who are basically autocratic in their approach to
handling people. Autocratic is the right word because this immediately
typifies this person's instinctive reaction to a decision-making situation. This is the person who cracks the whip constantly in order to get
things done, the person who relies upon his positional authority as
we have called it. He's the person who says, "I'm the boss and from
now on I make all the rules and decisions around here: you do what
I tell you because I'm supposed to know better than you, etc., etc."

On the other hand is the so-called democratic or developmental
kind of person. Developmental is perhaps a better term, not because
of my political affiliations but because of what the word means. If
you are a developmental kind of supervisor, manager, leader, you
are engaged all the time in trying to develop, to encourage the maturing process of those below you. Whereas if you are an autocratic
person, you couldn't care less what happens to their development or
maturing process; you just want to get a job done.

A word of caution is immediately in order. Despite the way the
preceding description of these two polar types seems to read, neither
one is all white nor all black. As a matter of fact, very often it is the
autocratic or control minded person, the one who believes in getting
things done because he has to meet a target, who really seems to be
accomplishing things. He's the one you find at the top of the list
whenever you read an account of those who meet their goal, who get
the production out, who raised the most money in a parish and built
the biggest plant and all the rest of that. Very often it is the fellow
who gets up there and makes everybody else "knuckle down," or
cracks the whip all the time who seems to get his job accomplished
and for that reason one is tempted to say there is nothing wrong with
this approach.

On the other hand you have the people who believe philosophically
that it is not only important to get a job done, but that the long range

[1] Douglas McGregor, excerpt from an unpublished speech.

has to be considered also. You have to think about this as an on-going organization. You have to ask yourself: What's going to happen if I should become incapacitated and my strong, firm control at the helm is no longer there? Will the group fall apart? If it will, then I'm being very shortsighted; so I must therefore concentrate on developing those below me. I must encourage someone to be ready to take my place. I must have a back-up. I must have key people who can keep this thing going even if I want to take a month's vacation in Florida, or whatever the reason might be.

Theory X and Theory Y

Douglas McGregor in his book, *The Human Side of Enterprise*, discusses these two styles of leadership under what he calls Theory X and Theory Y. Theory X generally is synonymous with the autocratic approach. According to this theory, ordering and forbidding is the best way to assure performance. People are considered as having little ambition and as trying to avoid responsibility in wanting to be told what to do. This leads the administrator to assume the responsibility for setting objectives and to exercise close control to see that these objectives are carried out. It fosters a relationship in which subordinates or followers are quite dependent upon you, showing relatively little self-expression or self-responsibility beyond what you specify.

On the other hand Theory Y is generally synonymous with the developmental approach. It is based on the assumption that to challenge people with real opportunity can encourage them to excellence of performance. It is the result of looking upon people as accepting and even enjoying their work and eager to accept responsibility. It leads to participation in the setting up of objectives and to the exercise of close control in such a way that people grow by broadening themselves. It fosters a relationship in which subordinates can be quite independent and self-reliant if their temperaments allow.

Notice how, according to these two theories, the actions of the administrator flow logically from his attitude or assumptions about followers and their capacity for development. Since the autocrat believes people dislike work and avoid it when they can; that they must be closely directed and controlled; that they don't want responsibility and are not interested in self-development; then he is prone to the following kinds of action:

1. He says little unless something is wrong.
2. He usually is not interested in the ideas of others.
3. He decides what information people need.
4. He changes his demands unexpectedly.
5. He is sometimes hard to talk to.
6. He discourages his people from taking risks.

Conversely, since the developmental administrator believes that people accept and enjoy work; that they can direct and control themselves; that they accept and seek responsibility and value self-development; then his consequent actions are likely to be:

1. He considers ideas that conflict with his own.
2. He allows a reasonable margin for error.
3. He tries to help others learn from their mistakes.
4. He has consistently high expectations.
5. He encourages people to reach in new directions.
6. He helps people understand the objectives of their jobs.

It must be realized that it is rare to find one or the other style of leader in the pure state, as it were. Administrators usually fall somewhere along a line from the pure autocrat on the one hand to the pure democrat on the other. As a matter of fact, we might more appropriately consider styles of leadership as being a continuum such as is represented by line A-D in Figure 5. The individual administrator can usually find his position along this continuum somewhere to the right or left of the midpoint M. If we dissect line A-D, at point M, we can probably describe those who fall either to the left or right of this dissecting line somewhat as indicated by the catch words in Figure 5.

1. If we are talking about an autocratic person, the one who cracks the whip, there is a small four letter word, a polite four letter word, which might be used to describe such a person. The word is "boss." Why is "boss" an appropriate word for such a person? Not simply because that is what a lot of you call your pastor! But probably because of the connotation behind the word. One immediately does not think of a pleasant person when he hears the word "boss." To the contrary one thinks of a firm taskmaster. One's lips even twitch or snarl when we speak the word. On the other hand what is a simple word to call a developmental kind of administrator? How about "leader"?

STYLES OF SUPERVISION		
STYLE:	A Autocratic M	Developmental D
Often called...	BOSS	LEADER
Motivates from...	FEAR	INSPIRATION
Supervision is...	CLOSE	GENERAL

FIGURE 5

That's a nice innocent sounding word. Nothing harsh about the term "leader." As a matter of fact, it seems to connote a little bit of empathy, a little bit of enthusiasm, a little bit of self-confidence when you talk about a person being your leader. He is someone you automatically want to follow because the word "leader" connotes followers, whereas, the word "boss" connotes something else completely.

2. Now how about their approach to getting things done? When the boss has a job to be done how does he go about getting it done, as regards giving instructions to people? He usually orders. Or if it is something he doesn't want done, he forbids. And to make certain that his wish is carried out he usually will dangle a threat when he forbids something or a carrot by way of reward when he orders something done. So the boss motivates out of fear, we say. He relies upon threats and rewards; he orders and forbids; that's the way he gets things done. What does a developmental type of person do instead? When he motivates, he suggests, he asks, he inspires, and here again we see the basic distinction between the two types of leaders, recognizing that when a person asks he does not lose control completely. This is the inspirational rather than the autocratic type of philosophy. By it people are shown why they should want to do what it is you want them to do.

3. Finally, the two types of leaders use a different procedure in the daily supervision of the work of followers. The autocratic leader gets involved in all the details. He tells people not only *what* to do, which

he should do as a decision-maker, but he also tells them *how* to do it, *when* to do it, *where* to do it; crosses every "t" and dots every "i," giving detailed instructions. Therefore, in Figure 5 we say he exercises *close* supervision over subordinates.

The developmental person, on the other hand, does not give the details of when and how and so forth. He stimulates the use of initiative. He delegates. He encourages the thought process of the person doing the job for him. He thereby gives this person an opportunity to mature; hence the word "developmental." In short, he exercises what is called *general* supervision; he gives the follower the ball, as it were, and tells him to run with it.

Paternalism or Laissez-Faire

A very specific application of styles of leadership which is present to a great degree in many parishes has to do with the paternalistic approach. This is the kind of leader, manager, administrator or pastor who thinks of himself as a real father. This is the autocratic person who handles people in a way that is cloaked with all that is normally considered to be sacred; this is what makes it so insidious. It does not appear that he is cracking the whip all the time. Quite the contrary; he is the fatherly type—he always has his arms outstretched. He is going to welcome people into his bosom at all times. But he does it in a way that he does not develop anybody because he fails to cut the apron strings. He keeps the umbilical cord wrapped so tightly around people that they are squeezed and shriveled up and finally are worth nothing because of this extreme paternalism. So the paternal approach which says, "Well, I'm really a nice fellow and there is no reason why my people won't come to me with their problems or there is no reason why anyone should be afraid to work for me because I'm not an ogre, I'm not a Simon Legree," simply avoids the fact that he is an autocrat and the people who work for him are not developed—they are stifled. And it is this concept of stifling their own growth, their own initiative, their own spirit of freedom that we talked about under the authority concept in the preceding chapter. That is the thing that is most common to all administrators who are on the left of center of our continuum A-D in Figure 5.

There is an extreme also, however, in the developmental or democratic approach. This is the style of leadership which comes close to being absence of leadership, anarchy, sometimes referred to as "the laissez-faire approach." When one goes too far on the developmental side, when one's invitation to participation borders on permissiveness, then there is danger of losing all control. One cannot go overboard on delegation to the point where he assigns the job to another and then absolves himself from the responsibility of following up. This is why in the quotation at the beginning of this chapter McGregor argued for balance in management so that there will be sufficient control to protect the results and objectives desired by the organization and yet sufficient freedom to permit growth and maturing and an atmosphere of mutual support.

Testing Your Own Place on the Continuum

Once we have a rather clear notion of what the two extreme types of leaders are we usually ask ourselves: What kind of leader am I? Do I have the tendency to be one way or the other? What side of the mid-point am I typically on? This is a difficult question to answer for oneself. It is even difficult for the man living with you in the same rectory to tell you the real truth of the matter. But business and industry have found a way of checking at least an instinctive *tendency* toward one extreme or the other. And a recognition of such a tendency would be a valuable asset for any priest-manager.

It would be valuable because in endeavoring to become an effective administrator one does not follow the same process he would follow in applying his learning of algebra or some other skill where he began with nothing. In this matter of dealing with people you do not begin with a blank slate; you begin with inborn instinctive approaches. For some way or other over the years you have already been dealing with people; you have already developed certain approaches in handling people. Therefore, what you must ask at this point is: Have I built up within me a tendency which I will have to counteract as I attempt to become an effective priest-manager? About the only way to test your typical patterns of behavior is to test the assumptions which we said earlier have a tremendous effect upon your consequent actions in dealing with people. What follows is a self-administered test devised by the Opinion Research Corporation, drawing upon their professional expertise in personnel psychology. This test will help you to determine for yourself which of the basic tendencies you might have, for whatever use you might find. If you find it of no use, if the test fails to work in your case because you are an exception, then just forget about it. But the test has been found helpful by the majority of those who have taken it in various walks of life, including over 900 priests who took it in formal sessions with the author.

There are only two simple ground rules for administering the test and they are as follows:

1. Since the purpose of the test is to determine your basic assumptions regarding people and hence arrive at an understanding of your proclivity in handling people, you should read each statement one by one and immediately put down your instinctive reaction by checking the appropriate column which most closely describes your position: do you strongly disagree, disagree, agree, or strongly agree? The idea here is not to deliberate regarding the statements, or try to determine what might be the "correct" answer for each statement. There is no right or wrong answer. Nor would it help to try to qualify your reaction. Simply check one column for each of the 15 statements.
2. When you come across the word "people" in the test, do not think of any particular individuals whom you have known in the past. Try to think generally of those who are the followers in your group.

The test should take no more than five or six minutes.

TEST YOUR OWN ASSUMPTIONS REGARDING PEOPLE AND THEIR WORK

(Check One)	Strongly Disagree	Disagree	Agree	Strongly Agree
1. Almost everyone could probably improve his job performance quite a bit if he really wanted to.	___	___	___	___
2. It is unrealistic to expect people to show the same enthusiasm for their work as for their leisure activities.	___	___	___	___

3. Even when given encouragement by the boss, very few people show the desire to improve themselves on the job. ____ ____ ____ ____

4. If you give people enough money, they are less likely to worry about such intangibles as status or recognition. ____ ____ ____ ____

5. Usually when people talk about wanting more responsible jobs, they really mean they want more money and status. ____ ____ ____ ____

6. Because most people don't like to make decisions on their own, it is hard to get them to assume individual responsibility. ____ ____ ____ ____

7. Being tough with people will usually get them to do what you want. ____ ____ ____ ____

8. A good way to get people to do more work is to crack down on them once in a while. ____ ____ ____ ____

9. It weakens a man's prestige whenever he has to admit that a subordinate has been right and he has been wrong.   ___   ___   ___   ___

10. The most effective supervisor is one who gets the results expected, regardless of the methods he uses in handling people.   ___   ___   ___   ___

11. It is too much to expect that people will try to do a good job without being prodded by their boss.   ___   ___   ___   ___

12. The boss who expects his people to set their own standards for superior performance will probably find they don't set them very high.   ___   ___   ___   ___

13. If people don't use much imagination and ingenuity on the job, it is probably because relatively few people have much of either.   ___   ___   ___   ___

14. One problem in asking for the ideas of subordinates is that their perspective is too limited for their suggestions to be of much practical value.　　———　　———　　———　　———

15. It is only human nature for people to try to do as little work as they can get away with.　　———　　———　　———　　———

A) Totals for Columns　　———　　———　　———　　———

B) Above Totals　　(×1)———　(×2)———　(×3)———　(×4)———

C) Grand Total　　———

Scoring and Meaning of the Test

A. Total the number of check marks in each column and insert these numbers in the appropriate blanks at the end of the test. Obviously if you have not skipped any statements, and if you have totaled correctly in each column, if you add the numbers that you are inserting opposite A you should get 15.

B. Next you are asked to multiply whatever total you have at the end of each column by either one, two, three, or four as indicated opposite B. Another way of saying this is that each check mark in the strongly disagree column is worth one point; each check mark in the disagree column is worth two points; each check mark in the agree column is worth three points; each check mark in the strongly agree column is worth four points. (Remember that any number multiplied by zero is still zero, even in the new mathematics!)

C. Your grand total is the sum of the four figures that you just arrived at in the row opposite B. This grand total should be somewhere between 15 and 60.

Before finding out what your score means, you should do one more thing. The purpose of this test is to place you somewhere on the continuum A-D in Figure 5. What do you think will be your position?

Do you think you will be somewhere to the left of midpoint: that is, that you are somewhat autocratic in your method of handling people? If so, place an X somewhere on the line to the left of the midpoint indicating how far over you think you may be. On the other hand do you feel you are somewhere to the right of center; that is, that you are developmental to some degree or other in your handling of people? If so, put an X mark somewhere to the right of center indicating how far over you think you are.

According to those who devised this test, as borne out by the many groups who have subsequently taken it, and about whom we had sufficient information to enable us to check the validity and reliability of the test, your score probably indicates something like the following. If you scored 39 or higher you are probably somewhat autocratic, that is, at least half-way between the midpoint and point A on the continuum. If you scored 29 or less, you are probably somewhat developmental, that is, at least half-way from midpoint to point D on the continuum. If you scored in between 29 and 39, perhaps there is still some hope for you!

Beyond this, what specifically should you be concerned with in regard to your score? Probably the following points are worth considering:

1. Did you get yourself on the right side of the midpoint? Does your score agree with your "guesstimate" of your position on the continuum? If you place yourself on the wrong side of center, then you may be in trouble; that is, you may not know enough about your own method of handling people.

2. If you are way out at the autocratic end of the continuum, that is if you scored somewhere between 52 and 60, then you are probably in trouble. This means you have very definite high-handed tendencies in dealing with followers. You apparently feel that people do not have much initiative of their own, that they have to be watched very carefully, that they have nothing to contribute of value to a group endeavor, that they are motivated by selfishness only, and that you therefore are constrained to be overbearing and too control oriented in directing their activities.

3. If you are way out on the developmental end of the continuum, that is, scored somewhere between 15 and 20, chances are you

are also in trouble. This is because you apparently do not have sufficient controls. You are perhaps too permissive in your approach to people and might well be living in the proverbial dream world of the naïve idealist.

4. If you scored a middle score, that is 33 to 35 or thereabouts, you could be in trouble. It depends on how you got there. If you have a middle score because you checked some answers in the first column and some answers in the last column, so that the pluses offset the minuses as it were, then you are probably in trouble. This is because you do not recognize the inconsistency in your responses. A careful rereading of the statements will indicate that all the 15 statements really say the same thing in a different way. Therefore, at the very least, you should be rather consistent in your replies. Answers running down the middle columns, even though they are labeled agree and disagree are not really inconsistent, given the rapidity with which you had to respond. But even allowing for lack of deliberation, your answers should not spread from strongly disagree to strongly agree on sentiments which are really the same.

5. Finally it should be pointed out that this test, like most similar tests which attempt to examine the preconscious level, is subject to wide ranges of validity for a given individual. Application of the laws of statistics will insure that in the majority of instances the test is proven reliable. However, there will always be individuals for whom it is not conclusive. For example, one priest who took the test under the direction of the author went straight down the first column, scoring 15 points. Discussion with him revealed that he had done advanced work in psychology and immediately recognized what the test was trying to measure and so he "beat the test." He is obviously atypical and the test was not really a test for him. There will be many others who will find that the particular conditions under which they take the test, not to mention the particular historical era in which we now find ourselves with its concomitant sudden awareness of the lessons being taught in this chapter, may serve to make them atypical also. The test is offered only as a help, only as an aid, it is not meant to be a sure-fire, foolproof, guaranteed psychoanalysis.

The Law of the Situation

A woman management writer around the turn of the century, Mary Parker Follett, spoke of what she called "the law of the situation." She was addressing herself to this matter of the best way to handle followers, and suggested that much of the personal bitterness that sometimes serves only to harm the interpersonal relations between those who must give orders and those who must follow would be eliminated if neither person should give the orders to the other but both should agree to take their orders from the situation.

This depersonalization of the order-giving process is the most important aspect of Follett's philosophy regarding the exercise of authority. She suggests that authority must be exercised but that in doing so it is really the authority of the situation and not the authority of the leader which will be respected by followers. She refers to this as "the authority of the fact." The idea is that when all parties concerned identify the same facts and the same goals, it is most common for them to make the same decisions. This is really the lesson we should take away from the test that we have just completed. There is no one right side of the continuum to be on. We are not, in this chapter, waving the flag for the democratic or developmental approach to the exclusion of any firm control or autocracy at all. The truth of the matter is that the individual situation, the facts, should determine the style of leadership to be used by the leader. When the situation at hand, the risk involved, the seriousness of the circumstances, are such that extreme care and precise following of orders is called for, then one wants to be on the autocratic side of the mid-point. However, when there is no great risk, when the quality of the decision will not be affected one way or the other, then there ought to be more latitude on the part of the followers and less control on the part of the administrator.

This obviously includes consideration of the makeup of the group itself and the style of leadership to which they have been accustomed. For example, if you are transferred to a new parish tomorrow and learn that your predecessor has ruled his flock with an iron hand, you might wish to relax the controls. If you take the position that, starting at once, democracy will be the rule of the day now that you are pastor, you may well be inviting catastrophe. It will do you no good to call everyone together and announce that from now on things are going to be handled in a truly democratic fashion, that you are going to put everything to a vote rather than issue the kind of orders and directives to which they have been accustomed. Were you to follow such a completely different tack from that of your predecessor, chances are the roof would cave in around your ears very quickly. The people just are not ready in such a situation for the degree of freedom which you hope to be able to give them. Prudence would dictate that you relax the reins gradually rather than make the immediate switch.

CHAPTER SIX

MANAGEMENT BY OBJECTIVES

The preceding three chapters have expanded on the significant ways for the priest-administrator to improve on his use of time. Knowing where one's time goes was identified in Chapter One as the first habit or practice of an effective leader. We are now ready to consider the next practice: effective executives focus on outward contribution, i.e., they are results-oriented. This has come to be known rather commonly as "management by objectives."

Countless successful administrators today feel that the most significant management tool to appear in a long while is the concept of "management by objectives"—MBO. This idea was first mentioned by Peter Drucker in his highly influential book *Practice of Management*, published in 1954. The thesis of this important work is that managers who plan the future of their organization are more likely to succeed than those who merely guide their enterprises without any attempt to shape their own future.

Since then, any management writer or lecturer worth his salt has subscribed to the idea that a true manager is one who "acts" rather than "reacts," who "makes things happen," rather than suffers things to happen. The *Harvard Business Review*, the American Management Association, the best known management development program—all have now joined in singing the praises of this approach.

As can be expected, however, this rather rapid universal acceptance has not been without its share of confusion. By now there are 57 or more varieties of management by objectives. Our purpose is not to examine each of these, nor even to choose the better from the worse. Our objective is rather to outline the concept of MBO which has proven helpful as an approach to management for several priest-managers (in parish work or in staff work) known to the writer personally.

Need for This System

The concept of MBO did not just happen. It was developed to suit a set of management needs. In order to understand better what the system now is, it is good to reflect first on what needs it was meant to satisfy.

1. Need for planning

Management by reaction is no longer adequate in our changing society. If an organization is to be successful—be it an industrial enterprise or a non-profit service organization—its goals and objectives must be planned to happen. This planning involves many individuals in a process of idea exchange.

What is needed, then, is a philosophy of organizing and planning that encourages and directs the work of everyone within the organization, knowingly, toward specific agreed-upon results that are part and parcel of the total results expected of the whole enterprise.

2. Need for improved motivation

Today's extremely busy world requires more attention to the management function of motivating followers, especially other supervisory people, if the weak ones are to be developed and the strong ones kept. Each person must feel involved in the development and implementation of the goal-attaining projects of the entire organization.

A system is, therefore, needed which involves each individual in establishing his own goals, even though they must be approved and perhaps modified by his leader. This is consistent with the following results of recent motivational research:

—Groups which are allowed to do their own planning are generally more effective than those given a pre-set plan of action.
—Individuals who are systematically encouraged and assisted in setting their own levels of achievement do significantly better than those who are not.
—Groups and individuals perform much better and reach planned objectives much more quickly when they are provided, on an

interim basis, with reliable and objective information on their progress.

—Use of carefully structured rewards will provide motivation for improvement at all levels of performance.

3. Need for more communication

Extensive research has shown that lack of communication between leader and follower lies behind the discrepancy between a worker's performance and his leader's expectations. Literally thousands of matched-pair comparisons were made, attempting to match up the job as the leader expected it to be done (including what he thought should be the standard used to measure performance of each task) against the job as the follower thought he was supposed to perform it (including his standards of measurement). In a properly organized operation, there should be a perfect match. However, ninety-nine times out of a hundred there is found to be an offset, some non-alignment. (See Figure 6) There are some duties which the leader expects the follower to be doing although the worker is unaware that these are part of his job. And there are some duties which the follower is performing about which the leader has no knowledge.

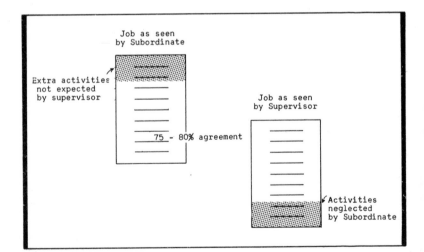

FIGURE 6

A management system should seek to detect and remedy any such condition as quickly as possible, by providing frequent opportunities for such matched pairs to compare notes in a face-to-face interview designed to relieve the tension that might otherwise attend such a confrontation.

4. Need for a systems approach

Organizations which are well provided with highly trained personnel, professionally qualified to carry out programs in their own field, or highly motivated out of apostolic zeal, often fail to achieve total objectives owing to an inability to coordinate the efforts of the various sub-units. While the professional may do an excellent job as judged by the standards of his own field of knowledge, his contribution to the total effort may be marginal because of his unwillingness to become a team member or his inability to subordinate his system to the superordinate system which comprises the whole organization.

The management team must, therefore, proceed on the basis of clarifying common objectives of the whole before delineating specific goals of subordinate units. At the same time they must provide a mechanism for fitting all the parts of the jigsaw puzzle together by using improved communications laterally as well as vertically.

Management by objectives was—and is—offered as a way to satisfy these needs. It is important to recognize that MBO is therefore a way of helping leaders do the things they *must* do if they are to be true managers. It is not an added burden, as some people are inclined to regard it, nor an optional "extra" that would be fine if we had more time for fancy frills. It is the best way we now know to do the job of being a manager.

With this orientation to the origin of the system and broad basis for recognizing its necessity, let us examine its worth for the priest-manager. To do this, let us first define it, then examine its relevant elements, and finally suggest a workable approach toward implementing MBO as a system in a parish. It should be remembered that the same approach can apply as well to other groups; we use a parish only as an example.

Definition of MBO

Management by objectives may be defined as a continual process whereby leader and followers in a parish periodically identify its common goals, define each individual's major areas of responsibility in terms of results expected of him, and use these agreed-upon measures as guides for operating each program and for assessing the contribution of each to the work of the entire parish.

Some will immediately—and correctly—point out that there is nothing new in this. There are no erudite phrases here, no new jargon to be learned, no sophisticated tools, such as operations research, requiring the employment of a staff of experts to help the pastor manage his parish. The system contains many old friends from the world of management. It speaks of levels of authority, delineation of responsibilities, delegation of power, setting of goals, use of control devices, determination of standards of performance, and evaluation of results. All familiar ideas, true!

But MBO puts them together in a different way. MBO systematizes things which all too often are done only on a hit and miss basis, if at all. Therein lies not only its novelty, but also its greatest attraction: its simplicity. It may require work, but it's the kind of work that everyone can understand without an advanced degree in management science!

If there is anything new at all in this definition, it is the special emphasis given to self-commitment. If MBO does anything, it *pinpoints* responsibility through the opportunity for *self-determination* afforded to followers. Now let us examine the six basic elements contained in the system.

Elements of System

1. Leader and follower AGREE on some important things

Because it is intended to get everyone in the parish working in harmony toward the same objectives, the idea exchange we are talking about must take place between every superior-subordinate pair.

One should have a mental picture, then, of the co-pastor as moderator of a parish society and the president of the men's club, as an example, sitting down in private to have this exchange of ideas. The system is based on this kind of a face-to-face meeting. And the first element stresses the concept of *agreement* as the philosophical underpinning of the entire system. It argues immediately for the style of leadership often called participative, permissive, developmental.

The agreement they arrive at, and the process of communication they use with each other throughout all that follows is a constant *sharing* of ideas. It comes from a willingness on the part of each to compromise. It may require each to bend a little from earlier positions. It might literally result in a "management contract" in which two levels of managers commit themselves to a course of action, to programs, to mutual understanding of each other's responsibilities and rights, just as in any other contract.

2. Common goals are agreed upon first

The first subject of discussion should be the common goals of the parish (or the smaller unit to which both belong; here, the men's club as the process is implemented further down in the organization). Before a person begins to talk about his own work, he ought to have a clear understanding of, and commitment to, the common goals or objectives (we are using the words interchangeably) of the whole group.

Motivation theorists tell us that people are much more reconciled to work expected of them if they see how it fits the total picture. Reason tells us we can make more consistent decisions if we have a frame of reference against which to measure any smaller problem affecting our own area.

Common goals here would include such things as:

—the objective of examining the purpose and functions of a men's club in the modern parish;
—the objective of revitalizing the club as an active body of militant men working on projects relevant in today's society;
—the goal of cooperating with neighboring parishes in a effort to influence city government to pass a fair housing law.

The type of agreement envisioned with respect to these common goals is not so much the result of bargaining over numbers, or even discussing yes or no, for it is assumed that common goals will have been determined prior to this meeting, as will be evident in discussing the implementation steps below. The agreement here is in the form of mutual acceptance and commitment to these common goals, not out of fear or subservience, but because a leader takes the time to explain the why's and wherefore's, knowing that the follower will then be better able to perform his part of the job.

3. Major areas of responsibility are defined

Having accepted as worthy of achievement the total goals of the group, the organization president is now ready to review his own role in achieving them. He will do this by suggesting what his major assignments are, and getting confirmation from the priest-manager regarding this.

These are generally broad areas of delegation, general duties which are pretty much defined in the follower's job description or list of functions. Typical things uncovered here include the absence of any written position guide, or the necessity for rewriting an existing guide because of changes in work expected (perhaps due to organizational changes), or a realization that no work at all has been done in the whole area of the position description owing to the press of other work. For example:

—Assume that membership has dropped to the point where only 80 men pay dues and only 30 attend meetings with any degree of regularity. It could be that the officers feel it is up to the priests to build up the membership; and perhaps the priests feel the men are supposed to take care of this through a membership chairman. Actually, each could have a valid point, but until they sit down and talk about it, they will more than likely have a Mexican stand-off.

—Or it could be that the men some time ago raised a considerable amount of money, planning to start a parish athletic fund. But when the money was put in the bank the pastor decided he needed it for teachers' salaries, and some of the men still feel they ought to be able to determine how the money they raise will be spent. This is simply a matter of clarifying the extent of authority and responsibility of each, and getting agreement on it, the sort of thing that is so often not discussed, but taken for granted by everyone (in opposing ways).

4. Specific targets are set for each area of responsibility

For each major task accepted by the club president, short-term, specific objectives are set. These are major work projects or improvements which are expected to be completed within a twelve-month (usually) period. These together make up the "performance budget" or plan for the coming year. Some important aspects of these objectives are:

—They must flow from the position description.
—They must be consistent with, and take their cue from, overall group and parish objectives.
—They must be measurable. The measurement of results against these targets requires the development of appropriate yardsticks. Time is one such measuring rod, but is not sufficient by itself, for it does not reflect the degree of achievement. Even pure service goals can usually be measured by quantity, quality, cost and time standards. This is the determination of "par" for the particular responsibility area. The standards set here really show what is "the acceptable level of performance." If the responsibility areas answer the question "What is my job?" the goal and standards answer the question "How do I know when I'm doing that job well?"
—Objectives must be challenging, if they are to provide motivation and a feeling of real accomplishment.
—At the same time, they must be attainable and reasonably within the control of the individual involved.
—Too many targets, however reasonable, will result in a loss of control. Experience shows a neophyte can handle about six goals rather well at first; ten to twelve can be expected after some practice.
—It will help to assign priorities, at least informally, in order to get agreement on rank of importance whenever difficulties regarding alternative courses of action arise.

The expression of a complete objective with all its measuring devices can be done following a suggested format which is explained with the help of a worksheet, such as the one shown on page 82. Examples will be given at that time.

5. These agreed-upon goals are used as a daily guide

Once agreement has been reached between the leader and the follower on the slate of goals, the planning ceases, and the controlling begins. If the goals are to serve as useful guides, they must not remain a verbal agreement, but should be reduced to writing. Then they should not be left to gather dust on a shelf, or locked in a desk drawer. They should be kept for ready reference just as any other contract spelling out performance commitments.

The president should refer to them for guidance in allocation of his personal time and energy and for distribution of the resources at his disposal. He should, every day and all day long, see to it that his energies are expended in pursuit of this slate of goals. He should literally do nothing that is not connected with the agreed-upon list of objectives, because, by definition, they constitute what *both* he and his leader agreed was his work assignment.

6. The list of objectives is the basis for a formal evaluation

If the follower works faithfully every day toward the accomplishment of his objectives, it follows that at the end of the "budget year" he is to be reviewed on the basis of his results in these areas, and not on some other less meaningful set of criteria. This is not the place to decry mistakes that are often made by the use of undefined personality traits, or abstract behavioral adjectives (often masquerading as very concrete point-scoring forms of self-hypnosis) in many of our appraisal systems.

The point here is that people have committed themselves to work

1.	Superior - Subordinate AGREEMENT
2.	Common Goals Accepted
3.	Major Areas of Responsibility Delineated
4.	Realistic, Concrete Goals Are Set and Standards of Performance Assigned
5.	Commitment to Use as Daily Guide
6.	Basis for Formal Evaluation

FIGURE 7

toward a set of objectives. They have literally staked their careers on achieving those goals inasfar as they could control their outcome. Then they should be assessed on this basis, which means a Results Oriented Performance Evaluation (ROPE) as the other side of the coin of MBO, its necessary aftermath.

How To Do It

A logical question at this point, assuming relative satisfaction with the outline of the elements of the system explained thus far, is: "Where do I start?, How do I begin?" What follows, then, is a workable four-step procedure for anyone who wishes to have the kind of face-to-face idea-exchange meeting we have just described.

STEP ONE. Clarify your working organization chart.

A necessary preliminary step to your meeting with the followers is a review of the organizational relationships that exist or should exist in the parish or the section of the parish which you manage. This means simply to take a piece of paper and sketch out roughly a chart showing yourself and *only* those reporting directly to you. Those farther down in the organization will be handled by their own immediate superior. For each person you indicate you should make a note of roughly what responsibilities you feel he should have, and especially which of the total parish or group objectives he is most responsible for achieving. Note also any pending changes in division of authority or responsibility you may have in mind.

STEP TWO. Review the performance record of each key subordinate.

A second necessary preliminary step is to go over the previous record of each follower on your list. This means examining his prior performance reviews, salary progress (if he is a paid employee), career mobility. It might mean checking the records of the personnel office in a school or talking to the man's prior supervisor or just plain doing some personal reflection. It takes time, but it should not be neglected.

The purpose of this preliminary step is to assess the man's potential to accomplish the kind of goals you (or he) might have in mind. You cannot do an intelligent job of setting performance standards, or even assigning work responsibilities unless you have taken stock of each of your followers. This is the management function of organizing. You are trying to build the strongest possible work team you can. In order to do this you must know the strong and weak points of the members of this team and then set objectives and standards of performance accordingly.

Peter Drucker says it is no longer a question of trying to find people who are good for everything—the question today is "Good for what?" He goes on to relate the story about Abraham Lincoln at the time he appointed Ulysses S. Grant to be general in charge of the Union Armies during the Civil War. Apparently the members of Lincoln's Cabinet came to him and said, "Mr. President, you can't be serious. Don't you know that man has a fondness for the bottle?" To which Lincoln is reported to have said, "If I knew what his brand of whiskey were, I'd send a keg of it to each of my generals!"

The point was that even though Grant had some weaknesses, his strong suit was winning battles and that was the kind of skill called for at the moment, so Lincoln intended to build upon that strength. You must do the same—not hire drunkards, but build upon the strong points of your followers!

STEP THREE. Have the idea exchange meeting.

a) Some days before you intend to meet, advise the follower of your wish to meet with him and ask him to prepare for it. Assure him of your undivided attention during the hour or so you have blocked out for this purpose. You must convince him of the importance of the meeting so that he will prepare for it well. Ask him to come prepared to discuss what he would like to set as his objectives for the coming year. Suggest that he use "Job Objectives Worksheets" (Figure 8 described below) as a guide. Give him a copy of your objectives so he will take his lead from you and will have an early awareness of common goals with which his must be consistent.

b) Prior to the meeting, you also should be preparing. You should be ready to discuss with him the goals *you* think he should be ready to commit himself to. Your preparation is as necessary as his, if the meeting is to be a true exchange of ideas. If you go there with a mind so open that it is empty, chances for meaningful discussion are minimal.

c) At the appointed time have the meeting, obtaining a commitment from the follower regarding the level of performance in each responsibility area. Here it is important to practice all the usual leadership skills in conducting interviews. He must bear the initiative, for it is his meeting; but you must insure a fruitful outcome by encouraging him to set his own standards for excellence of performance, if at all possible.

d) Before the meeting comes to a close, remember what some authors call the golden rule of management. Say to the subordinate, "What can I do to help you accomplish this objective?" Reasons for this should be obvious. It's all a matter of recognizing that if his goals spring from yours, as they should, if you have delegated to him a portion of your own authority, then in a sense helping him to achieve his objectives is contributing to the attainment of your own. In the final analysis you are measured by how well he reaches his goals, so you ought to be anxious to help him.

e) Make two copies of the final agreement. He keeps one and you keep one. You each want a copy because once again this is a contract, and you have each committed yourselves to certain actions, so you need a copy to refer to.

STEP FOUR. Review your set of followers' budgets occasionally.

How often you review them will vary with your span of control. This is the follow-up phase of the system. No plan in the world is any better than the follow-up attention it receives. Furthermore, objectives should not be strait jackets which prevent freedom of movement as time passes. Should changing circumstances warrant modification in objectives, there must be an opportunity to do so— provided the change is made bilaterally, just as the original goal was made. Hence, you must check periodically to see:

—Are you keeping your commitment to the follower in assisting him to reach his goals?
—Is he making progress according to the standards of performance you both agreed upon?
—Should the goals or standards be modified?

Examples of Complete Objective

A well written objective will always include four things: 1) a brief statement of the goal itself in measurable terms; 2) a detailed plan

```
┌─────────────────────────────────────────────────────────────────┐
│                    JOB OBJECTIVE WORK SHEET                       │
│                                                                   │
│  Name:_____    Position:_____ │
│                                                                   │
│  Responsibility Area:_____    For Budget Year Ending:_____ │
│                                                                   │
│  Background Information:                                           │
│                                                                   │
│                                                                   │
│                                                                   │
│                                                                   │
│                                                                   │
│                                                                   │
│                                                                   │
│  Objective:                                                       │
│                                                                   │
│                                                                   │
│                                                                   │
│                                                                   │
│  Program Element   Yardstick or Indicator   Standard (Results Expected) │
│                                              Minimum │ Average │ Maximum │
│  1.                                                                │
│  2.                                                                │
│  3.                                                                │
│  4.                                                                │
│                                                                   │
│  etc.:                                                            │
│                                                                   │
│  Pay-off:                                                         │
│                                                                   │
└─────────────────────────────────────────────────────────────────┘
```

FIGURE 8

of attack, or method for achieving the goal; 3) a timetable, to include intermediate checkpoints; and 4) a statement of the results expected.

To arrive at these four items it is necessary to consider several other things also. Figure 8 shows a sample worksheet which can be helpful in arranging such additional information in a logical fashion for purposes of analysis. It is suggested that a follower take each of his major responsibility areas and complete a worksheet for them, one by one.

To show how this might work, let us return to the example of the co-pastor discussing objectives with the president of the parish men's club. They have agreed that the president will be responsible for maintaining the level of membership where it should be. Now this is to be *his* duty, and it will be written into his list of functions, not to change from one year to the next.

But what would be a satisfactory level of performance in carrying out this job function this year? They must now agree on the target for this year, and on how this goal is to be achieved. Following the worksheet in Figure 8, they might agree first of all on certain background information, which might be worded as follows:

> There are 1000 families in this parish, with a potential membership of 1000 for the men's club. Subtracting the usual ⅓ who either never join anything, or are unable to attend meetings because of night work, etc., there is a possible membership of 667. We had an all-time high of 400 members when the parish was relatively new and spirit was high, and this would be considered a very satisfactory number at this time, given what we know about membership levels in such organizations everywhere else. Most recent figures show 80 paid members and 30 attending meetings regularly. This has been so for the past two years, due generally to lack of interest.

Notice that this information should include: 1) explanations of present happenings; 2) causes for present state of affairs; 3) statistical or other measurement of present level of activity; 4) some reason for wanting to change or improve; 5) any additional constraints that might have to be kept in mind.

Then the president would make a brief statement of his intentions or goal, e.g., "to increase membership and active interest in meetings and programs." This rough approximation will be refined to include specific measurements before it becomes a final objective, but this is just a worksheet so far.

To achieve this objective, a step-by-step plan of attack, or approach to the problem, must be worked out. Each step should have some indicator (at least a time schedule) to show that the program is moving according to schedule. The pay-off parts of the program will also have their yardsticks broken down into *minimum* acceptable level, *average* expected level, and *maximum* desirable level. Our example might look like this:

1) Conduct survey of men of parish to determine reasons for non-membership and their desires for the club before they become members.
   Yardsticks: time to complete: 1 month from now
   type of survey: telephone contact by officers to every 5th home on parish roster
   results expected: to receive some definite answers to questions
   minimum: from 50% of calls
   average: from 66⅔% of calls
   maximum: from 90% of calls

2) Brainstorm ways of approaching men with meaningful appeal to join and participate.
   Yardsticks: time to complete: monthly meeting after survey
   volume of ideas deemed presentable by officers: minimum: six; average: ten; maximum: twenty

3) Have priests present new appeals from pulpit and in parish bulletin.
   Yardsticks: frequency: four Sundays in a row before membership meeting in the Fall
   content: use copy prepared by president

4) Officers to follow up survey by calling back all the homes originally contacted to give new appeal.
   Yardsticks: time to complete: during some 4 weeks prior to Fall membership meeting
   volume: complete calls to: minimum: 50% of families; average: 66⅔% of families; maximum: 90% of families

5) Repeat steps 2, 3, 4 in the Spring with different families.
   Pay-off

	Min.	Ave.	Max.
Increase in paid members Fall	120	160	200
Increase in paid members Spring	200	240	280
Increase in attendance by Christmas	75	100	120
Increase in attendance by Easter	120	150	175

The president is now ready to restate his objective in a complete manner as follows: "Objective: an increase in membership for the Fall drive from the present 80 dues paying members to 120–200 and in the Spring drive to 200–280; and an increase in regular attendance at meetings from the present 30 to 75–120 by Christmas and to 120–175 by Easter."

It will be noted that in setting the standard of performance a range is always given rather than a single figure. There are three reasons for this:

1) To overcome the temptation to "pad the figures" by the leader. There is a definite tendency on the part of leaders to add a safety margin when they assign work. If a report is due on the 10th of a month, they'll delegate it and say it is due on the 5th. If they must raise $10,000, they will say they need $15,000. If they would be pleased with a membership of 120, they will ask for 200. While it is a good idea to have a protective margin for safety, it should be identified as such. Using the range concept, the leader is able to ask the follower to aim at the upper extremity (200 members) but also admits he will be satisfied with the lower extremity (120) which is set at the *minimum acceptable level*.

2) To provide a challenge for the follower. Just to offer the minimum acceptable level, or even the average, would not stimulate the best efforts from the workers on a project. The rise of a range holds up to their eye a more challenging target, while not crushing the weaker ones who might see the upper extremities as unrealistic.

3) To provide an opportunity for distinguishing among those who do minimum work, average work and obviously superior work.

Arguments Against MBO

Among the most frequent objections encountered in this writer's attempts to install MBO are the following:

1) "It takes too much time." It is true that *some* time must be spent in learning to discipline oneself to think logically, to plan consistently, to present an argument cogently. That it takes *too much* time is debatable. Priest-administrator executives, like others in industry, government service, education and all walks

of life, put a premium on time, and rightly so. But very often, if the truth be faced, the lack of a system like MBO costs *more* time in ineffective operations and solving crises when the panic button is pushed than it would have cost to plan correctly in the first place. It is probably the hard work and discipline itself, not to mention the fear of committing oneself to preplanned results that is usually behind the time objection.

2) "Not everyone can handle such a sophisticated approach to being a manager." Because of the various levels of sophistication that are present among our priest-managers it will be important for you to handle each interview according to the ability of the individual. Some are strong leaders, perhaps with a scientific background, who are used to thinking and planning systematically and they will have little trouble merely formalizing their thoughts according to this particular format. Others are the weaker managers, especially those who in everything else show they are pretty much "working supervisors," and they will need patience, encouragement and help. But you should avoid doing the job for them, setting their goals for them precisely because they *are* weak. This process is an excellent tool for the development of such managers. They can be brought along in the ability to plan and solve problems and set meaningful goals, if you don't expect miracles overnight and don't give in to the temptation to spare them the embarrassment of their first faltering steps.

3) "As long as objectives work from the top down, we are back to autocratic imposition of work from above." Figure 9 shows how there is really a cyclical process taking place, so that the leader's objectives are set with full knowledge of the wishes and capabilities of the rest of the parish. At stage 1, the leader is constantly asking others in the parish for information, for evidence about needs and opportunities, about strengths and weaknesses. It would be a poor administrator who planned his total goals without first assessing the resources available to carry them out.

Stage 2 is composed of *a*) the formulation by the leader of total goals, taking into account not only the information available from below, but also the pressures from above, i.e., the community, the diocese, the government, accreditation agencies, etc.; and *b*) the

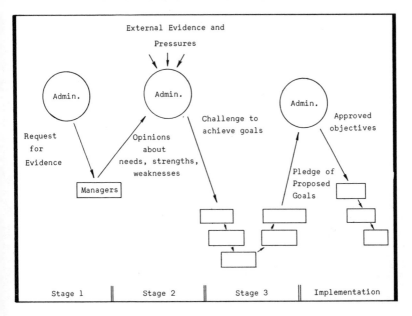

FIGURE 9

issuance of these total objectives as a *challenge* to the rest of the organization, and not as a tyrannical set of directives.

Stage 3 consists of followers presenting their goals and objectives first as pledges, willingness to commit themselves, and then after discussion with the leader as a contractual agreement, so there is total commitment by all going into the implementation phase.

Installation of MBO Parish Wide

What is to be described here is the procedure followed by this writer as a consultant in working with several organizations of varying sizes and types to install the system of MBO.

Basic Assumptions

1. Managerial personnel (clerics as well as lay) have frequently demonstrated technical competency in their field of specialty; but very often do not exhibit the same assurance in management skills.

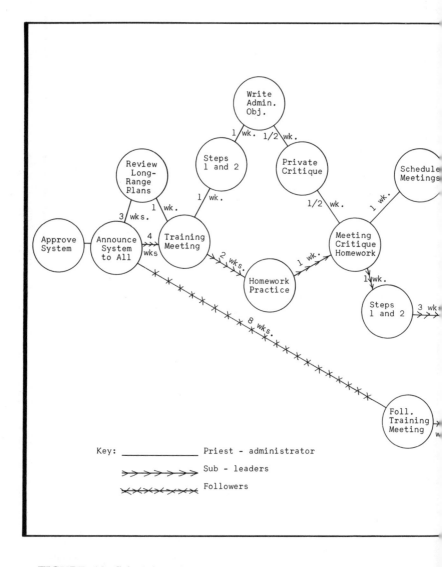

FIGURE 10. Schedule to install systems of MBO.

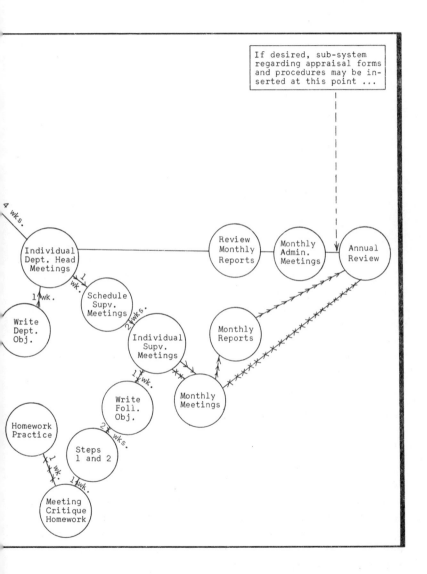

2. Their formal and informal knowledge of management and management skills is quite limited because their exposure to professional management concepts has been sporadic and unstructured.

3. There is need of a uniform and carefully planned approach to the task of managing the parish as shared by all supervisory personnel.

4. The exigencies of time dictate that supervisory personnel must pretty much learn the art of managing as they conduct their daily work.

5. There is a recognition that today's supervisor is faced with the challenge of learning to achieve objectives through the work of others, i.e., learning to be a manager.

6. The system of management known as MANAGEMENT BY OBJECTIVES appears to provide the kind of catalyst needed to give a sense of direction to all activities and programs within the parish.

7. Selection of acceptable control devices to insure progress toward the achievement of objectives, and as a constant means of communication between levels of authority would be helpful.

8. Use of approved evaluation techniques in measuring job performance, recognizing satisfactory achievement and correcting behavior for the future is necessary.

9. Review of the system in order to increase sharpness in setting objectives until all personnel achieve a satisfactory level of expertness must be done.

Scheduling the Installation

In Figure 10 the various steps to install the system have been arranged in a schedule to illustrate how they are linked together. Beginning with the first training meeting, it can be seen that the system is actually a single cycle repeated three different times, once for each level of authority—pastor, other leaders, and followers. The cycle consists of training in the system (to include individual practice and review training) followed by preparation of one's objectives as a pledge and discussion of them with one's superior.

How To Do a Performance Review

As the first step in getting ready for a performance review, it is necessary that you and each of your subordinates be agreed upon what is expected in terms of results. For each management position there should be a statement of conditions which exist when a high level of satisfactory performance has been attained. This was done when you set the objectives.

Using this statement of objectives, ask the follower to prepare for the discussion by thinking through the results which he is getting, a few areas in which he can do even better, what will be required for this improvement, and what you can do, refrain from doing or do differently which will help him improve his results.

Schedule a time and place that will be convenient, private and comfortable for the actual performance review. Allow plenty of time for the discussion. Avoid interruptions and don't hurry.

Think through in objective terms what you expected of him on his present job. What results is this man getting? How is he doing in each area of responsibility? Are there areas in which he is doing too well to the neglect of other important functions? Make notes of specific examples for discussion of accomplishments and areas for improvement.

Think through what you are doing to help him improve performance. What more can you do in delegation, communications, coaching, facilities, stimulation and recognition? What are you doing that impairs his performance?

Determine what needs to be said during the discussion: the opening, the most effective approaches, the possible reactions (yours and his). Tailor your approach to the man and the situation. Get ready to listen with interest and understanding.

Then have the discussion. Let the person know that you consider this discussion important. Be sincere, natural and businesslike.

Seek understanding of yourself, the man, your mutual relationship, objectives, goals and responsibilities. Consider accomplishments, problems and areas for improvement. What *results* are being obtained? Save discussion of promotion, potential and career for another time.

Listen attentively. Encourage him to talk and to ask questions. Make the person's *current performance* the central subject.

Ask him to discuss the areas he has selected for improvement. Have him discuss how he plans to improve on each. Later, ask him how he thinks you can help him improve. When you both agree on what can and should be done, make notes of the plans, goals and objectives for your and his use later.

Ask him what you as his leader could do, refrain from doing or do differently which would help him do an even better job. Don't ask him what is wrong with you. Don't go on the defensive or argue. Don't ask for examples. Look to the future, not the past. Nearly every subordinate has ideas concerning how his supervisor could help him, but if he does not express them, wait a while and then try some questions that may bring out suggestions; for example, "How could I improve on recognizing jobs well done?" "What additional authority do you need to meet your responsibilities?"

Discuss your impressions of his performance on each group of his responsibilities. Start with those where improvement is needed. End with those on which he is doing an outstanding job. Use examples. You may find it desirable to alternate between functions on which improvement is needed and the ones which have been outstanding. Concentrate on a few areas for improvement. Avoid the "fine, but . . ." technique.

Avoid using or thinking in terms of "weaknesses," "faults" and "shortcomings." Concentrate on results and actions but avoid discussion of personality traits, peculiarities and attitudes. Especially avoid dwelling on isolated incidents or mistakes of bygone years.

Compare each man's performance with the standards for his present job. Do not compare one man with another. Avoid using yourself as an example. Judge operating results.

Keep open-minded. Be willing to change your viewpoint or even the way you do things, but do not tell others how they should be different.

Be careful in giving advice. Avoid such approaches as "If I were you . . ." or "If you did this . . ." or "Why don't you . . ." Encourage each person to work out his own plan for improvement. Help him develop insight into the reasons for his behavior and the consequences of his actions. Use questions that stimulate thinking, but avoid leading questions.

Be cautious in making promises. Keep the ones you make.

Review the points agreed upon. Be sure you have made notes of the important points, particularly plans for improvement, objectives and targets. Whenever possible, let the man put the conclusions in his own words, with each of you having a copy for follow-up. End the discussion on an encouraging note of confidence. Schedule a follow-up meeting and make it clear that you will be looking forward to further discussion and improvement.

Continually capitalize on every one of your performance reviews by putting into effect the agreed-upon plans for improvement, by following up on all plans frequently and by re-planning whenever necessary.

Recognize progress and keep interest alive. Keep currently informed concerning what each of your followers wants to do, can do and is doing.

Keep having informal discussions of performance, progress and results as often as possible. Try meeting at the other person's place of work, or at least on neutral ground.

Face up to failures.

Continually strive for higher standards of performance for yourself and for the individuals in your group. Keep yourself and your group improvement-minded and stretching toward definite objectives.

Set an example by your own performance and by your methods of managing.

To summarize the review:

STEP ONE.   Near the end of the year ask each man with whom a performance budget was set to prepare a brief "Statement of Performance Against Budget," using his copy of the performance budget as a guide. Tell him:
    a) Don't rewrite the whole statement, just a verbal (numerical if possible) estimate of your accomplishments compared with targets.
    b) Give reasons for variances.
    c) List additional accomplishments not budgeted.

STEP TWO.   Set a date to go over this report in detail. Search for causes of variances.
    a) Was it your fault?
    b) Was it some failure on his part?
    c) Was it beyond control?
    d) Get his agreement on just how good his performance was and where he fell down.

STEP THREE.   Cover other things on his mind. If he's so disposed, turn to other things he might want to talk about. These might include relationships on the job, opportunity, job related personal problems, etc. Don't rush this. If he'd prefer, set another date for this.

STEP FOUR.   Set the stage for making his Performance Budget for the coming year.

A final helpful device in beginning the practice of setting objectives is to recognize that there are three types of objectives, corresponding to the three ways of spending time discussed in Chapter Three. Some of our time involves routine or repetitive operations (those that keep the wheels turning); and some of our time is taken up with putting out fires (solving problems); and some of our time is spent on creative projects (innovations). It would follow, then, that some of our objectives ought to be for routine matters, some for problem solving, and some for innovations. The method described in this chapter is most applicable for routine areas and innovations. A special approach for problems will be the subject of the next chapter.

Bibliography

DEEGAN, ARTHUR and O'DONOVAN, THOMAS. "Mow Much Authority Should an Administrator Delegate?" *The Modern Hospital*, October 1964.

DEEGAN, ARTHUR. "Management by Management," *Management of Personnel Quarterly*, Spring 1967.

DRUCKER, PETER. *Practice of Management*, Harper and Brothers, New York, 1954.

MAHLER, WALTER. "A Systems Approach to Management by Objectives," *Systems and Procedures Journal*, Sept.-Oct. 1965.

McCLONKEY, DALE. *How to Manage by Results*, American Management Association, New York, 1965.

ODIORNE, GEORGE. *Management by Objectives*, Pitman, New York, 1965.

SCHLEK, EDWARD. *Management by Results*, McGraw-Hill Book Co., New York, 1961.

CHAPTER SEVEN

PROBLEM SOLVING AND DECISION MAKING

Hundreds of books and many thousands of pages have been written about problem-solving and the decision-making process. It might be supposed that the nature of this process would by this time be generally agreed upon. Yet, despite renewed efforts at clarification (often brilliant in their insight) by distinguished scientists, philosophers and business executives, universal agreement concerning the nature of decision-making is still lacking.

Ultimately, it is the judgment of the manager or leader, based on whatever evidence is available, which dictates a decision. If his judgment is too precipitous, if it ignores accumulated evidence, if it is not based on the lessons of experience, such judgment can be fatal. Recognition of the fact that good decision-making is based more on a philosophy or attitude than on any specific techniques, coupled with adherence to a few fundamental principles, will eliminate much of the human error in the process.[1]

A prime prerequisite to appreciation of the proper philosophy or attitude for decision-making and a necessary preliminary to a fruitful study of the problem-solving process outlined in this chapter is a clear understanding of the scientific method and its more important elements. The science of management simply as a body of knowledge is of no use to the priest-manager. Only when he acquires this science as a habit does it become valuable to him. However, even then his knowledge could remain fruitless if it is not fertilized by the complimentary art which will help him in its use.

[1] Attention is invited to the recent development in scientific decision-making of the use of scientific electronic computers, through which as much as possible of human judgment is replaced by the inexorable conclusions of a given set of data fed into the machine.

The *art* of decision-making enables one to bridge the gap between knowing how a job should be done and actually doing it. Art is action-oriented; it is related to strategy or the combining of assets in an optimum way. In decision-making it must always be the artful supervisor who must use the knowledge he acquired scientifically to make the choice which only a human will make. Knowledge will always be the handmaid of the will.[2]

Characteristics of the Scientific Method of Decision-Making

First, the discriminating decision-maker recognizes that every result has a cause and seeks a natural explanation for observable phenomena. He accepts realistically the causal interrelationships of events in the world of administration. He does not trust to chance as a competent means of providing for the success of his venture. He refuses to follow the trial and error method of determining correct decisions as being expensive, time consuming and again oblivious to the cogency of observable experience.

Second, the critical decision-maker learns to generalize from past experiences. Even irrational animals, when repeatedly confronted with an identical set of circumstances which have proven harmful in the past, learn to generalize from laws of association and attempt to avoid these dangers. For example, the dog can soon associate the sound of a buzzer followed by a slight electric shock, so that after a few instances, when he hears the buzzer, he cringes from the anticipated shock. This is generalizing in its crudest form.

Third, the scientific minded decision-maker rejects authority (in the sense of an expert on a given subject and not direct line supervisory authority) as the basis for making a decision in favor of observation. He adopts an "I'm from Missouri" attitude and takes nothing for granted or merely on someone's say so. The only authority he recognizes is a publicly verifiable experiment.

Fourth, the mature decision-maker recognizes the limitations of pure logic and abandons the attempt to reason out decisions in a vacuum from which all pertinent data are excluded. He realizes that

[2] See, for example, Thomas Aquinas, *Summa Theologica* I-II, question 57, Article I, where it is held that even the so-called intellectual virtues are, strictly speaking, not virtuous, because of themselves they are fruitless. They require an act of the human will to bear fruit.

premises can often times be erroneous, leading to faulty conclusions. He is aware of the difficulties of semantics which all too frequently can lead one man to illogical conclusions from someone else's principles.

Fifth, the precise decision-maker goes beyond mere observation to exacting experimentation when possible. While any observation is more scientific than an unfounded estimation, the skilled problem solver is trained in the choice of relevant factors, delicate instruments, mathematical calculations and verifiable sequences, as the best way to a scientific constant and hence to the most fruitful administrative decision.

Limitations of Scientific Decision-Making

The discriminating administrator also realizes the limitations of any scientific approach to decision-making and weighs these in its use. Among these limitations may be mentioned the following:

First, the scientific decision-making process will not solve all human problems. Dealing mainly with phenomena of the natural or physical sciences, it is not applicable to the less quantifiable factors which frequently are important in the handling of human beings and their problems. When the human will, personality, character, likes and dislikes, etc. are relevant factors, even the most conclusive scientific conclusions must be considered only tentative or as mere guides.

Second, time does not always permit the full decision-making process. Because of limited time available before a decision must be made it is sometimes necessary to curtail the complete investigation into facts and to make the best possible judgment. Complete validity of the scientific approach is predicated on the ability to test all possible variable factors. Any contingency for stalling completion of such testing limits to that extent the reliability of the conclusions reached. Time is but one such contingency. Others include too great expense, the inaccessibility of certain required data and the like.

Third, there are also limitations on the part of those who use this method. Their perceptions and abilities may not be developed to permit maximum results. The elements they work with are often numerous and highly complex. Then too, they may have difficulties in correcting personal bias in carrying out their tasks. This would tend to color all conclusions with the outlook of the individual rather than allow objectivity. This may even be because insufficient knowledge is available to recognize the bias.

Fourth, haphazard events may occur which could not have been anticipated. This complicates the process and prevents the full advantages from being obtained.

Fifth, closely allied to the preceding limitations is the difficulty sometimes encountered in perceiving the significant data and/or creating proper decision-making situations. This could be the result of physical limitations, reasons of a time-space dimension or even humanitarian sentiments.

Defining Problems as a Part of Setting Objectives

The scientific approach to decision-making as described above is probably not totally unfamiliar to you, as most courses in philosophy provide some exposure to it. A different version of it, based on the management system discussed in Chapter Six, probably is new and would provide a significant aid in handling many of the decisions which must be made in the daily life of the priest-manager.

Since most decisions, at least the difficult ones, seem to involve problems, it will be helpful to discuss this topic as a technique for solving problems. In the management by objectives approach to problem-solving, there are four basic steps: definition of the problem, identification of possible causes of the problem, brainstorming alternative solutions for the problem, and selection of a course of action after analysis of probable outcome for each alternative.

1. *Definition of the problem.* To define anything means to set its limitations, to spell out its configuration. The first step in problem solving is to do precisely that. Too many people try to solve problems before they have reduced them from a vague feeling of uneasiness to precise and measurable outlines. To do this, the following process is suggested:

a) Identify the problem area. For example, "Not all parishioners are using their Sunday envelopes"; or "Too many people are coming in late for Mass"; or "It's difficult to keep teachers in our school." These are probably all valid problem areas, i.e., reasons for the priest-manager to be concerned. But so far, he can do nothing with them. He is not even sure how alarmed he ought to be about them. Most problems, when sufficiently boiled down, lend themselves to analytical measurement.

b) Apply Pareto's Law (the 80/20 Rule). This is to add further identification to the problem area, by extracting the most significant sub-problem. Vilfredo Pareto, a 19th century Italian engineer and economist, noted that a very large percentage of the wealth of the country (represented by the 80 in the 80/20 Rule) was held by a small percentage of the people (the 20 in the 80/20 Rule). It might actually be 90/10 or 75/25, but whatever the precise figures, the observation has been found to be true in countless situations, so the "law" says that the important items in a given whole usually constitute a small portion of the total.[3]

The priest-manager can apply this rule to his situation by examining his problems and, instead of trying to solve a vague, broad problem (cure-the-world's-ills approach), he can be practical and go for the greatest gain by identifying the crucial few (20%) who or which are responsible for the greatest number of times (80%) the problem occurs. For example, are all parishioners coming in late to Mass or is it usually the same steady offenders at certain Masses? (Therefore, instead of biting criticism from the pulpit aimed at all, steps will be taken to deal with the few who are causing the problem.) Again: is it hard to keep *all* teachers in our school, or does the turnover seem to occur primarily in certain grades, or for certain classrooms, or in certain subject areas?

c) Statement of present level and reasonable desired level. The problem becomes ultimately defined only with the identification of

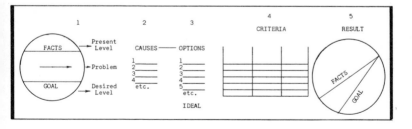

FIGURE 11

[3] C. Jay Slaybough, "Pareto's Law and Modern Management," *Management Services* (March-April 1967).

the present level of activity in the problem area vis-à-vis a desired level of activity. These two measurements may be graphically considered as the present *facts* and the desired *goal*, as shown in Figure 11. In this way, the problem finally is seen as the difference between the present facts and the goal. It is thus an obstacle, something to be removed or eliminated, so that the new facts will come together and meet the goal ("result" in Figure 11).

At this point, both where you are (present level) and where you want to go (desired level) are meaningfully defined. This enables you to make two important judgments:

1) Is the problem really big enough to make it worth the expenditure of time and effort? This question assumes a belief in real problems as significant enough deviations from desired results-level to cause people to want to bear the cost of changing them. For example, if the problem being considered is the non-use of Sunday envelopes, and the present level is 50% of registered parishioners never using them, whereas a reasonable desired level (based upon usage in comparable parishes locally and nationally) is 30% of registered parishioners never using them, then the problem is really seen as the difference (20% of registered parishioners) and may really be worth some time and effort to correct. But if the present level is 31% and a reasonable desired level is 30%, then the management problem is only 1% of registered parishioners, in which case perhaps it is *not a problem about which you can hope to do much*, so you might better devote your time to other areas.

2) This allows the second judgment, namely, where is this problem to be placed in a hierarchy of priorities? Most of us have more than one problem at a given time, yet we have a limited amount of time, money, people to use in solving problems. It then becomes important to allocate these resources most effectively, i.e., where the return promises to be greatest.

2. *Identifying possible causes.* Having clearly fixed the scope of the problem and determined that it merits attention, the next step is *not* to consider how to eliminate it, or solve it. Experience proves that problems cannot be attacked head-on. Even though the goal is to eliminate the problem as an obstacle, this can be accomplished only by determining the causes for the problem and eliminating them, i.e., attacking the problem at its root. Therefore, step two is to make an exhaustive list of contributory causes of the problem.

Here the problem-solver is called upon to use his understanding of the true nature of the problem and how it comes about. But he is not thereby left "to his own devices." He will find it helpful here to use creative techniques such as "brainstorming" and other partici-pative methods of involving his associates in the decision-making process. Here too he will find it useful to keep the 80/20 Rule in mind, and begin to sort out those causes which account for the great-est part of the problem.

3. *Listing alternative solutions or optional courses of action.*   Since there is always more than one way to skin a cat, the chances are that the problem can be solved in more than one way. Too many people are likely to try the first solution that comes to mind, and when that doesn't do the whole job, try another way, then another and another, until by trial and error they stumble across an acceptable method. Scientific decision-making teaches us to analyze the many possible ways first and then try the one with greatest likelihood of achieving our goal.

In trying to come up with options, it will help to recall that you are looking for "cause eliminators." Hence Figure 11 shows that "causes" lead to "options" (indicated by the arrow). As a rule each contributory cause brings to mind one or more possible courses of action that will eliminate at least that one cause of the problem. At this stage, it is usually helpful to list all possible solutions that come to mind, without yet analyzing their likelihood of success. (The brain-storming technique recommends not pausing to weigh the merits of ideas as they come to mind, lest the creative, imaginative interactive processes be impeded from producing further ideas.)

4. *Analyzing alternatives and selection of course of action.*   Some people believe the way to solve problems is to "try everything," to cover all bets, as it were, and thus "be sure something happens." The trouble with such an approach is that even if it does succeed in correcting things, it is impossible to know what is working for you and what is working against you. Trying several solutions at once is a kind of "shotgun approach," an uncontrolled experiment. Managers who consistently get results prefer to run *controlled experiments*: a single, specific strategy is selected and applied (the high powered rifle approach). The degree to which it fails or succeeds acts as a guideline for modifications resulting in future controlled actions. Thus we seek a *choice-situation* rather than just a *problem-situation*.

Examination of many controlled experiments on a wide array of management problems indicates that success comes most frequently when the course of action chosen meets the two or three common criteria of low *cost*, high *feasibility*, and high *contribution to objectives*. Other criteria could be selected in analyzing the options to find the one (or two) best courses of action: e.g., time to implement, effect on morale of organization, etc. The point is: some criteria should be chosen, inserted in Figure 11 in the appropriate place, and then a judgment made about each option for each criterion.

Once the matrix is filled in, the option that comes closest to matching a hypothetical "ideal" solution is the one which should be put into action. This approach prevents second-guessing or working by intuition. It is the discipline of the system which dictates the course of action to be pursued.

Of course, the system is only as good as the problem-solver's ability to evaluate each option against the criteria. Hence, again it will be helpful for him to use the team approach in weighing the alternatives. Associates with differing points of view or areas of responsibility in the group will usually help prevent bias in judging feasibility, contributions to objective, etc.

Practical Illustration: Improving the CCD Program

A practical example or two of how this problem-solving technique has been used by priest-managers might make the steps described above take on real meaning. While it will be impossible to set down all the reasoning that took place, the following will serve to put life into the different parts of Figure 11.

Assume you are in charge of the high school CCD program (religious education program) in the parish and you feel you have a problem in attendance. (Not too difficult to imagine!) Following the process outlined in step one, you consider all the facts and learn there are 550 high school students who should be attending. There are 220 registered in the CCD program. There are 180 who come regularly. You realize that 100% regular attendance of those eligible is not realistic. You feel 80% is much more like a realistic ideal, based on what you know from your own past experience and that of surrounding parishes. Figure 12 shows your understanding of the scope of the problem at this point.

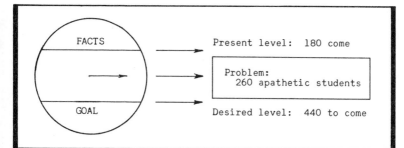

FIGURE 12. CCD Problem: Step One: The Problem.

Next you seek contributory causes: you ask *why* the 260 students are not coming. You draw on your own experience; you seek counsel with other priests; you talk to parents of students who are missing; you meet and interview students themselves, both those who attend and those who do not. Figure 13 shows the list of causes you come up with.

```
1.  Incompetent teachers making program distasteful.
2.  Insufficient budget to provide improved program.
3.  Unattractive and poorly written books.
4.  Disjointed program:  no continuity from year to
      year so students say "I've had that before."
5.  Competing demands on students' time: some work
      evenings; some have homework; entertainment.
```

FIGURE 13. CCD Problem: Step Two: Causes.

Step three calls for an imaginative approach to listing possible action steps which will eliminate the causes of the problem. Using the same participative approaches mentioned under causes, you think of the possible solutions indicated in Figure 14, each of which can be seen to be connected with one or more causes.

Step four involves choosing appropriate criteria and analyzing the options against these criteria to select one which comes closest to the ideal. You decide to use contribution to objective, cost and feasibility as the main criteria, but you also feel "appeal to young" is especially important here (even though it is implicitly included in contributions to objective). You choose a simple scale of HI-MEDIUM-LO, and

1.	Typical program with a variety of teachers to reduce the monotony.
2.	Typical program, but introduce electives as a means of increasing appeal.
3.	Make the program a monthly meeting for each student of 2-3 hours, to stress its importance.
4.	Use creativity in publicizing the program and doing a real "sell" job on students.
5.	Change the time from a week day evening to Saturday A.M.
6.	Recruit a core of parent/youngsters to seek out the apathetic one by one.
7.	Allow students to enroll in the program by putting together groups of their own choice to discuss problems they feel are relevant.
8.	Use more team planning to provide interest, continuity, and progression in content manner.
9.	Hire progressional teachers.
10.	Buy improved, attractive texts.

FIGURE 14. CCD Problem: Step Three: Options.

in the matrix in Figure 15 you fill in the "ideal" as HI in contributions to objective, LO in cost, HI in feasibility and HI in appeal to young. You then proceed to make a judgment about each of the alternatives and complete the work sheet.

OPTIONS		CRITERIA			
OPTIONS		Contribution to Objective	Cost	Feasibility	Appeal to Young
1.	Teacher variety	LO	LO	Med	Med
2.	Electives	Med	LO	Med	Med
3.	Monthly program	HI	LO	HI	HI
4.	Publicity	LO	Med	Med	LO
5.	Change time	Med	LO	HI	Med
6.	Individual approach	LO	LO	LO	LO
7.	Groups	HI	LO	HI	HI
8.	Team planning	HI	LO	HI	Med
9.	Professional teachers	HI	HI	Med	HI
10.	New texts	Med	Med	HI	HI
IDEAL		HI	LO	HI	HI

FIGURE 15. CCD Problem: Step Four: Analysis.

Of course, the particular facts of the parish would lead you to make your analysis one way or the other. What you had decided were more significant causes probably had a good deal to do with how you rated your alternative solutions under contribution to objective. (When you score one high here, you are implicitly saying it eliminates a highly significant cause, part of the 20% responsible for 80% of the problem.)

In many cases, as indeed perhaps in this problem, you may not say LO in cost is the ideal, because you realize one must at times bear added expense if he is to achieve his goal. Or, you may leave the ideal as LO in cost, but decide to weight the criteria such that a match in contribution to objective is worth 3 or 4 times a match in cost.

You are now ready to examine the chart and see which option is called for because it matches the ideal. Here, options 3 and 7 match perfectly and the recommended solution might be a combination of these two.

Practical Illustration: Integrating a Parish Altar Society

Assume now that you are moderator of the parish altar society and you feel as a group it is not Christian in its racist attitude toward minority members of the parish. You are in a rather small (600 families) parish which is changing in racial makeup. The altar society has only 40 members, but even though the parish is now over one-fifth Negro, there are no Negro members of the society. You feel that at least nominal integration by having two registered Negro members would go a long way toward improving race relations in the parish, so you set as your goal for the year having two Negro ladies in the society.

In the interest of saving time and space, Figures 16, 17, 18 and 19 give the salient information about how this problem could be analyzed, following the method used above. The reader is left to follow the process himself.

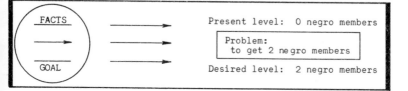

FIGURE 16. Altar Society Problem: Step One: Problems.

1. Long-standing racist attitude - outright lack of Christian charity or simple acceptance of minority group.
2. Militant anti-negro leadership of society.
3. Lack of any actual association with negro members of parish as basis for forming judgments.
4. Refusal of officers to seek negro members.

FIGURE 17. Altar Society Problems: Step Two: Causes.

1. Series of sermons and bulletins educating membership on Christian responsibilities to pave way for voluntary action by society members to invite negroes.
2. Priest to invite negro ladies to attend meetings as guests until ice is broken.
3. Priest to invite negro ladies to join at once.
4. Priest to disband society and reform it with new officers and open membership.
5. Pickets and demonstrations at society meetings protesting segregation.

FIGURE 18. Altar Society Problems: Step Three: Options.

OPTIONS	CRITERIA			
1. Education program	Med	HI	LO	Med
2. Guest	Med	HI	LO	LO
3. Immediate membership	HI	HI	HI	LO
4. Disband and start over	HI	LO	HI	LO
5. Pickets	LO	Med	Med	LO
IDEAL	HI	HI	LO	LO

FIGURE 19. Altar Society Problems: Step Four: Analysis.

Other Examples

Other problems which have been subjected to this kind of analysis in workshops with parish priests include the following:

—how to comply with a regulation limiting number of students in the parish school classrooms;

—how to develop information for a diocesan priests' senate regarding salaries for the clergy;

—how to raise funds to support a building program;

—improving the state of maintenance and repairs of the parish plant;

—securing the services of an organist;
—how to accommodate more children in school without doing more building;
—reducing interpersonal tensions existing in the rectory;
—increasing lay participation in the new liturgy;
—improving communications between priests and laity in a parish;
—developing a better Sunday Mass schedule.

CHAPTER EIGHT

MANAGEMENT OF THE PARISH

Examination in the preceding chapter of methods of effective decision-making concluded discussion of the five habits of the effective priest-manager enumerated in Chapter One as:

1) improving the use of one's time;
2) concentrating on results;
3) building on the strong points of associates;
4) focusing on the crucial few;
5) making effective decisions.

Those who possess these habits and practice them have demonstrated that they can be effective managers in a parish setting. Those who are still acquiring correct administrative patterns of behavior should look to assistant priests and talented members of their congregation for assistance. Yet research into the managerial habits of pastors in a 14-state area found many priests opposed to the use of assistant pastors and laymen in helping administer the parish.[1] Many of these same priests were the very ones who stated that demands upon their time for the accomplishment of administrative tasks often left them too little time to devote to the more spiritual matters for which they felt they were professionally trained.

Is this wise on their part? This chapter attempts to answer this question by correlating the extent of pastors' efficiency with the extent to which they do or do not utilize the services of available clerical and lay members of the parish, i.e., by delegating to them parts of their administrative responsibilities. After examining findings from

---

[1] A. X. Deegan, *Study of Career and Administrative Patterns of Pastors* (MBA thesis, University of Detroit, 1963).

such a correlation study made by the present author, suggestions and recommendations will be offered for the parish priest who wishes to compensate somewhat for his lack of formal training in management.

I. SUMMARY OF A RESEARCH STUDY

Nature of Study

In order to test the hypothesis that there is a positive relationship between the efficient operation of a parish and the use by the pastor of competent lay advisors or assistant pastors in a subordinate line or staff capacity, an in-depth examination was made of the management of 18 big-city parishes.

"Delegation of authority" was used to mean a pattern of behavior whereby a pastor would give assistant pastors or qualified lay persons actual decision-making powers in certain areas (at least over details) and/or rely upon them for advice and consultation that went beyond the "rubber stamp" variety. The term "efficiency" was meant to embody both the idea of getting results and also the most economical use of all available resources.

Ways of Measuring Delegation in a Parish

Ten practices were chosen to measure the extent of delegation by the pastor. Some had to do with more easily demonstrable activities on his part, while others were more related to his "philosophy of using assistant pastors and lay persons." However, in every case, evaluations of the pastor were made by considering his *behavior* in some way. The following is a list of the ten practices, which are offered here not only to report research findings, but as suggested norms which the reader may wish to apply to his own pastoral behavior.

1. Commitment to policy of using laity to share in administration;
2. Practice of assigning areas of responsibility to lay persons;
3. Practice of assigning areas of responsibility to assistant pastors;
4. Practice of utilizing church committees as advisors;
5. Practice of establishing other administrative *ad hoc* committees;
6. Practice of giving decision-making powers to committees;

Practice of Delegation	Number of Pastors
Commitment to use laity	14
Lay responsibilities given	12
Use of Church committees	10
Use of other committees	14
Sharing decision-making with committees	5
Assistants given responsibilities	8
Assistants in administration	12
Implementing changes	12
Managing by objectives	5
Attempts to overcome communications gap	8

FIGURE 20. Number of Pastors Found to Have Each of Ten Practices of Delegation.

7. Practice of inviting in and involving assistant pastors in administrative duties;
8. Implementation of recent changes in church operations;
9. Practice of managing by objectives;
10. Attempts to overcome "communications gap" in the parish.

In order to ascertain patterns of delegatory behavior, it is interesting to note which practices were found more often than others, and why. Figure 20 indicates how many pastors were found to have each of the ten practices. The dotted lines in the table indicate logical groupings of the subjects as they were discussed in the research study and as they will be discussed in the next sub-section.

Implications of Practices of Delegation

The first two habits relate to the pastors' practice of delegation to individual lay persons by sharing responsibilities with them in theory and in certain practical areas. The next three habits deal with delegation to committees of lay persons: the official Church committee (in some areas known as Board of Trustees) which is required by law, other committees of the pastor's choice, and finally decision-making committees as opposed to advisory groups. The third group of habits are the two related to the pastor's delegation of responsibilities to his assistant pastors. The last three habits are miscellaneous.

1. *Commitment to use laity.*   Because there is a danger that this is the socially acceptable thing to do today, the question of whether he favors using the laity in administration must be presented to the pastor as a projective test, i.e., to try to reduce the influence of the obvious value position included in this question.[2]

The major deterrent to this practice is an unwillingness by some pastors to accept the lay person in an auxiliary role. It seems to be a question of the credibility of the lay person. Some pastors view the

---

[2] The reader may test himself by asking himself which of the ten quotations which follow reflects closest his own belief:

1. "It is hard to find competent men. No one has the interest of the parish at heart as much as the pastor."
2. "Most parishes could profit greatly by increased utilization of the business and professional ability of many men in the parish."
3. "This parish has had outstanding success—mostly because the layman is given a chance to do something and he does it."
4. "A clique of laymen or laywomen tries to run or dominate parish affairs."
5. "If the pastor decides who is 'competent,' we are back where we started."
6. "My main task is to get out of their way and let them build the place."
7. "A middle-of-the-road course should be followed. The pastor should have some voice, but I believe the talents of the layman should be used more than they are at the present time."
8. "It is extremely difficult to pick the right lay people. They may be very efficient in their field—they are good fellows outside of parish work; but in parish work, if they become overbearing and a headache to the pastor and to the people, as does happen, it causes friction not only with that individual but also with his relatives and friends."
9. "Many of the laymen have the savvy that can save the parish hundreds of dollars."
10. "The laymen have shown themselves unreliable and nonpersevering."

modern emergence of the layman as a personal threat. They recall historical events when some unenlightened laity sought complete control of the Church to the exclusion of the rights of the pastor. Some leading lay persons today speak the same way. One interviewee stated categorically, "I disagree with the Vatican Council that the laity ought to take over the Church."

In order to correct this notion among the laity and to dispel the untrusting attitude among the pastors, there must be an intensive program of education as to the true role of the laity in the modern Church. Clarification of the proper roles of all actors was mentioned by the Vatican Council as among the first things to be accomplished.

Perhaps this charge of the Council has provided a new selling point for the hesitant pastor. There are those who argue that the major goal is for each segment of the People of God (clerical, religious and lay) to fulfill its proper role, and that efficiency is beside the point. They will not back a movement to encourage efficiency; but they will favor a move to have each person play his proper role. If it should turn out that the proper role is a reassignment of duties in a way that brings about greater efficiency, then the advocates of each will have their way.

2. *Sharing responsibilities with the laity.*   Many pastors indicated they would probably seek more opportunities to share their authority with the people in the parish, but were unfortunately not adept at securing acceptance of positions of responsibility when they were offered, due to the voluntary nature of most of the "assignments." It appears to many clerics that each parish has a small number of old "reliables" who can be counted on to do their part, and who are always the ones sharing the delegated powers. When asked what they encounter when they try to broaden the base of the number of those who might help one pastor expressed it bitterly: "What should I do: ask 30 who will say No, or go directly to the one upon whom I can count to say Yes?"

The fact is, however, that participation by subordinates is not necessarily a golden rule which must be followed at all times. This has been demonstrated time and again in industrial situations, leading Tannenbaum and Schmidt, among others, to observe that the choice of a leadership pattern is not made once and for all, and used in all situations. These authors reduce the decision regarding a style of leadership (basically a choice between some form of authoritarian rule and a more participative approach) to a consideration of three things: "forces in the manager, forces in the subordinates and forces in the situation,"[3] If the makeup of the subordinate advisors or the specific questions under discussion are not such that the subordinates would contribute any help to the decision-making process, then participation by them may be more harmful than helpful *in that instance.*

Other authors in the field of industrial psychology will be found a source of fruitful suggestions for the religious executive who wishes to learn the techniques of participative management.[4]

Again, some priests believe they are doing a great deal of delegating and sharing of responsibilities, but this is in areas which the laity regard as unimportant. The latter think in terms of meaningful assignments. They do not feel that being responsible for baling newspapers in a paper drive or selling tickets to a card party is really sharing in the administrative burden of managing a parish. "No one likes these dirty jobs," said one. But someone has to do them; and if they can be assigned in a way that shows how this frees the pastor for other responsibilities, there will be greater agreement.

Examples of areas where pastors have expressed satisfaction with the advice given by lay persons include: setting teachers' salaries, setting the amount of school tuition, hiring bookkeepers, hiring lay theologians, determining the method of raising parish income, timing of expansion projects, choosing architects and renderings.

Examples of areas where complete responsibility was turned over to lay persons satisfactorily include: management of a magazine-book rack in the church vestibule (with a turnover of over 700 items a month); manning a parish registration desk in the vestibule of the church, thus saving the time of the priests in the rectory; handling the school athletic program and/or school buses; obtaining bids and supervising installation of a paved parking lot.

One method used by one of the pastors in delegating to his lay persons is to stress what he calls the "unit of work concept." He

[3] Robert Tannenbaum and Warren H. Schmidt, "How to Choose a Leadership Pattern" (*Harvard Business Review*, Vol. 36, No. 2, March-April 1958), pp. 95–101.

[4] For example, Eugene Jennings, *Anatomy of Leadership* (New York: Harper and Brothers, 1960); Edwin A. Fleishman, editor, *Studies in Personnel and Industrial Psychology* (Homewood, Illinois: The Dorsey Press, Inc., 1961); Robert A. Sutermeister, *People and Productivity* (New York: McGraw-Hill Book Co., 1963).

tries to assign projects one by one as small problems that have to be solved. For example, if it's a question of finding a way to put up a fence around the bicycle parking area in the school yard to curb an increase in bicycle thefts, that is a special unit of work assigned to someone with no other responsibilities. This makes it easy to know the limitations of the man's duties and does not impose too much on the free time of very busy lay persons. It also helps the pastor who finds it hard to understand how he can delegate by suggesting that he break the work down into very small units, where it is easy to see how some of them can be turned over to others.

One very special question which arises in the area of using lay persons concerns the desirability of retaining the services of a lay person as a parish "business manager." It is suggested by many that such a paid parish employee be used to handle all the details of planning and administering a budget, counting and recording contributions, physical plant planning and maintenance, personnel policies and the like.

Those who favor the hiring of a lay business manager argue this way: the pastor, to be a shepherd, cannot concern himself with routine clerical duties which unfortunately do require some degree of decision-making; e.g., in the purchasing area. At the same time, the assistant pastor should not have to worry about material affairs. Therefore, a lay person, above the level of a clerk, should be the one involved in day-to-day business matters. He would be the one to hire a new janitor, to negotiate with Blue Cross about insurance claims, to talk to the local police about alleviating the traffic jams outside the church every Sunday morning. In major decisions, the pastor would have to participate. It is impossible to buy another priest, at any price: so why not spend $12,000–$15,000 annually to free some time for the present priests? He should be able to save his salary many times over.

The mean estimated salary for such a person was $10,000–$12,000. The comment most often made by pastors was: "We cannot afford such a luxury." A greater number favored the alternative of an older (perhaps semi-retired) person requiring less compensation, or a shared-time business manager who would be responsible for three or four parishes simultaneously. Even then, however, many pointed out the dearth of people appropriately trained for such a position.

Another fear of some pastors was that it would be difficult for them to allow the lay business manager to perform his duties without encroaching on his authority because of the novelty of the situation, but this was not deemed insuperable.

The major reason for opposition by lay respondents was the certainty that most parishes would have sufficient trained volunteer talent to accomplish the same result without paying for the services. This sentiment conforms with what professional fund raisers frequently find when called by a pastor to assist in raising parish income: a number of the lay members of the parish prefer to use voluntary help and "do it themselves" rather than pay for professional help. More often than not, this occurs in the more well-to-do parishes, so that it is not strictly a question of having the money available.

No lay people in this study agreed with the fear expressed by some pastors that the members of a parish would resent supporting one of their number by their voluntary contributions were the parish to hire a business manager.

3. *Use of Church committees.* Thirteen of the eighteen pastors interviewed said they not only had appointed an official church committee, but used it at least as an advisory body in administrative affairs. The other five readily admitted the committee was appointed merely to comply with the letter of the law. One reason given for this was that most questions to be decided by such a committee have been gone over time and time again with the appropriate diocesan office, therefore instead of wasting everyone's time with these questions, the pastor felt it was best to go directly to the diocesan office and get a decision there. Another reason was that approaching the men as individuals often got more honest answers, so that committees as such seemed to have no functions.

When the lay persons were questioned about how the pastors used the Church committee, fifteen of them thought they were not advisory at all. They referred to the functions of the committee as: "To sign the financial report on New Year's eve each year and have a quick drink with the pastor." (Signing the report is the one duty spelled out in diocesan regulations for members of the committee. Other functions are left to the discretion of the pastor.) Very often the chancery was blamed for not allowing them a greater role.

Reluctance on the part of the pastor to use his Church committee was attributed by many pastors to animosity dating back over 150 years to an earlier period of American Church history marked by bitter anti-clericalism, in which some lay persons attempted to seize control of Church property and establish a practice of "lay trusteeism."

4. *Use of other committees.* The purpose for including this habit is to inquire into delegation in some area outside the Church committee, thus showing how the pastor might avail himself of the chance to share his administrative burdens, according to his own needs. Examples of such committees are: fund-raising, plant and maintenance, heating, school board, youth, high school feasibility, etc.

As a rule these committees think they have less authority than the delegating pastor means to give them. There is one parish group (actually the largest single fund-raising group in its parish) whose accounts are handled by the secretary in the rectory office. The inability of the group to handle its own funds (deposits, checking account) is a sore spot with them, and an indication to them of how little authority they really have.

Typical of many pastors' manner of using these advisory bodies is this statement of one pastor: "I ask leading questions to get the men to suggest the things I want."

Greeley refers to this penchant of priests who use their charm for the purpose of manipulating people.[5] Many pastors manipulate their people, maneuver them, decide what is good or bad for them, when they ought to be providing a climate in which they could do their own deciding. The distinction between manipulating people and creating a climate of freedom may, in practice, be a very thin one. The only way a priest can tell whether he is doing one or the other is by asking whether his people are growing freer and more independent through their relationship with him or whether, as time goes on, they are becoming more dependent on him, more in need of his advice, more inclined to turn their decision-making over to him.

Very often the fact is that the pastor feels he is supposed to have these committees of advisors but does not know how to use them. One pastor offered an example of a policy area where his professional lay people could be used to advantage: What are we to do when stock is given to the parish? Some GM stock was given to the sisters in his parish school to buy equipment. A broker advised turning in

[5] Andrew Greeley, *The Hesitant Pilgrim* (New York: Sheed and Ward, Inc., 1966), p. 79.

the stock since the market was going down. The sisters wanted to "pray it up"!

5. *Sharing decision-making responsibilities with committees.* As will be recalled from Figure 20, this practice was tied for the lowest incidence with one other practice.

The pastors who did not purport to share decision-making steadily insisted that the role of committees and individual advisors was strictly to render advice. As one pastor phrased it: "The minute I am told I must share my decision-making authority with them is the instant when I turn in my resignation."

The reasoning behind this statement is that the pastor is solely accountable to his ecclesiastical superior, the bishop, and therefore he alone should have the entire responsibility of making decisions. As the person bearing the entire burden, he does not wish to risk letting others share in making decisions.

This finding is in agreement with a major finding of a survey taken of all priests in the subject diocese in 1965. The purpose of that survey was for the bishop to determine what channels of communication could be opened in the diocese among bishop, priests and laity. All 900 priests in the diocese were queried. Over 90% responded. Regarding the point of letting others share in responsibilities, the summary report of this survey states:

> Some suggested that the laity be given real responsibility, which includes accepting the possibility of their making mistakes just as this possibility exists for the priest in charge. Many reactions on this point in the survey indicated that a pastor who has an attitude of sharing responsibility will be able to avoid an overly paternalistic attitude that tends to regard the laity as children who cannot think for themselves.

Others have watched recent changes in other cities, e.g., in Pittsburgh, Pennsylvania, where the laity have been given greater decision-making powers, and say they do not want to start anything that will lead to "that kind of abuse."

Of the pastors who believed they did share this power while their laity felt they did not, the typical sentiment of the lay persons was: "He calls us decision-makers, but in reality we rubber-stamp his decisions or he gets a new committee." One interviewee recounted a decision regarding the architecture of the new church where the pastor had the committee reconsider its decision seven times until it saw the answer the same way he did, and then referred to the choice from the pulpit as "The men's wish."

One experienced pastor defended this action on the grounds of not wanting to be caught "in the middle" of an argument between the wishes of his people and the regulations of diocesan officials. His solution was to impose what he believed to be the norms of the chancery on his committee before any discussion could take place.

The parishes where committees did share decision-making authority were generally those where the pastor strove to improve the Church committee concept by enlarging its size and functions. Their thinking is reflected in this statement by one of them: "My expanded Church committee is my right arm. They think of all kinds of things I would never think of. We have never had a real disagreement yet. Since I am committed to letting them help make decisions, we all know the others have to be convinced so we work at it until we agree on a decision."

As for lay persons themselves: many are very uncomfortable in meetings where they might have a share in the decision-making process. As a result they do not act efficiently in them and cause dissatisfaction among fellow laymen as well as in their pastors. One layman recounted an incident when a group argued for one and one-half hours about putting screens on the church windows without coming to a decision, owing primarily, he said, to hesitancy to arrive at a decision known to be contrary to the desires of the pastor.

Pastors also mentioned that they sometimes wonder at the wisdom of spending untold amounts of time deliberating matters with a group of people when the same decision could be arrived at more speedily if the pastor made the decision unilaterally. They view this as an inefficient use of time. There is need of a greater realization of the trade-off of time for harmony and participative management and greater overall efficiency in the long run.

In one parish where the participation of the laity in the decision-making process appears to be rather well advanced, a layman described his pastor thus: "The little things he lets us take care of and we have learned to do a fair job of them. Real knotty problems we turn over to him, but at times he won't take the problem—he wants to save the democratic way, and so he won't bail us out of tough places. And really we respect him for that, because it would destroy the system if he took over."

Parish councils. Because of the insistence of Vatican II that diocesan and parochial councils be created, special comments on the implications of these bodies are called for.

One parish council already in operation works like this: the board is advisory in nature; monthly meetings are held; agendas are determined by the pastor and only these things are discussed. Members are at liberty to suggest items for discussion in advance. The discussions are not formalized into a Roberts Rule of Order motion-vote procedure. The pastor is not bound by any motion that is made by the board. The members say they can discuss things a lot more freely if they know the pastor can override any suggestion they make and that they will not have to declare themselves for him or against him by virtue of a formal vote.

Greeley suggests that this type of a council is sometimes derogated as "just" consultative.[6] Yet this type of consultation plays an important role in the preliminary steps of any decision-making process—the information-gathering steps. It would help provide some of the facts needed as a basis for a decision; it would serve to furnish some of the implications of the facts at hand; it would shed light on how other people interpret the facts; it would provide alternatives for consideration; it would especially indicate how the elite among the followers of the group viewed the entire matter. All of these are crucial preliminaries to the arrival at a decision. Those who share in these steps *are* sharing in the decision-making process. True, they do not *make* the final decision, but in no hierarchical structure can anyone but the administrator actually make the final decision.

It is the researchers' opinion that more lay persons like those interviewed in this study should understand the relationship between the data gathering and final stages of decision-making. There would then be a greater appreciation for consultative roles in decision-making and less denunciation of those who do seek preliminary advice but recognize that, close as information gathering and decision-making are, there comes a point where one stops and the other begins.

On the other hand, pastors might do well to see the full implications

---

[6] Greeley, *op. cit.,* pp. 93–94.

of their role of authority. There is more to authority than giving orders. One important facet is the function of promoting the most intelligent kind of participation possible for all members in the work of the group. Maier had clearly defined both these aspects of the role of the decision-maker when he distinguished between the two features of a decision which he identified as the *quality* element of a decision and its *acceptance level* on the part of those who must carry it out.[7] According to the multiplicative relationship he posits between these two, the wisest possible decision intrinsically must sometimes be put aside in favor of one which, though somewhat less perfect in itself, has a greater likelihood of being effective because of the greater degree of acceptance on the part of the followers owing to their having had a share in arriving at the decision.

As in all attempts at participative management, it is essential to safeguard the quality of the decisions that will eventuate and also the true representativeness of the members of the decision-making body.[8] Opinions varied widely as to the best method of assignment to the council. Some wanted parish-wide elections; some favored a "ward" or "block" representation method: some clung to the idea that the pastor would not agree unless he appointed the members. One man said the parish is not a democracy, and so the council should be appointed just as the President of the United States appoints his cabinet.

But others oppose this as the formation of a "clique" of cronies the pastor feels safe with. Rather, they say, a parish council will be effective only with a real system of subcommittees reporting back to the central body. In this way the true potential of the whole parish can be tapped. The pastor as one man cannot follow up the people who are constantly "blowing hot and cold," but a central committee can do this. Their main job is to keep the subcommittee people fired up enough to get a job done.

Most interviewees oppose the general election approach. They believe there are factions in all parishes and a general election will eventuate in divisions along these factional lines. They prefer nomination from among those who are known to be willing to work, and not

---

[7] Norman Maier, R. F., *Problem-Solving Discussion and Conferences* (New York: McGraw-Hill Book Company, 1963), pp. 3–5.

[8] Cf. Douglas McGregor, *The Human Side of Enterprise* (New York: McGraw-Hill Book Co., 1960).

desirous of the position for the prestige involved or to help their business, followed by area elections.

One detailed plan for accomplishing this consists of four steps: 1) block representatives are selected by the pastor to come to a general parish meeting to explain what will be done; 2) these block representatives return to their neighborhood and relay the information they received to their neighbors; 3) each block duly elects its permanent representative; 4) from these block representatives enough council members are elected at large to fill the positions open.

A diocese other than the one under study here conducted a series of modified Phillips 66 discussion sessions among a total of 4000 adults, in October of 1966, as part of a massive study program on the *Constitution on the Church* of Vatican II. In the summary report of the content of 2308 suggestion cards which came from these discussions, the section on parish administration contains the following points which touch on much of what has been mentioned here:

1) The parish council should be elected not appointed. Here the fear is expressed that an appointed council would be a rubber stamp of all viewpoints of the parishioners.
2) The parish council should be composed of men and women.
3) Men and women of special competence in legal, financial or school affairs should receive special consideration in election of members.
4) The main focus of the council will be on the financial and business affairs of the parish so that the pastor will be free to fulfill his spiritual duties more effectively.

It is interesting to note that parish councils are almost always suggested as a means of freeing the priest from non-priestly duties so that he may devote maximum time to spiritual needs. It is rarely insinuated that parish councils would do a better job of administering the parish finances. Most cards simply state that, while the layman is competent to help, his talents are not used in this area.[9]

6. *Assignment of responsibilities to assistant pastors.* Several reasons were mentioned by the interviewees as to why there seemed to be less delegation of administrative duties to clerics than to lay persons. Most often cited was the feeling that most assistant pastors are

[9] *Adult Education Report, A Study on the Constitution of the Church, by Renewal through Vatican II*, Lansing, Michigan, May 1, 1967.

already overburdened with responsibilities of a more spiritual nature, and that lightening the load for the pastor by transferring the burdens to the other priests was no improvement of the situation. Delegation was viewed by these respondents as the process of "getting rid of headaches" and relieving the clergy of all concern for things material. According to this definition, it was logical for them to feel that if any delegating was to be done at all, it should be done to the laity. But some of them were not sure any delegating would be done to start with, because of a desire "not to lose control" of the financial controls.

Assistant pastors explained the low rate of delegation in this area as a readily understandable reluctance of the senior clergymen to empower their juniors with any more authority than they had to. Where a pastor said he did delegate to assistant pastors and the assistant pastor said he did not, it was usually a question of the assistant pastor claiming he was given some responsibilities in name only— that in actual practice he had no authority to carry out the assignment. Prime concern here was in the monetary area. Younger clerics felt they could not really have responsibility even in the areas of sports or catechetical instruction, if they needed special permission to spend a nickel in these areas.

This finding is in agreement with a major conclusion of the priests' 1965 survey previously mentioned. The summary of the "Personnel" section of this survey stated:

> The need to find structures to make possible a full sharing of responsibility between the pastor and the assistant pastor is . . . in the emphasis given to the need for making more clear in the rectory situation that the pastor and assistant pastor share common goals and common responsibilities, and that each must be free to carry out his responsibilities creatively and imaginatively.

The general feeling among pastors was that assistant pastors are very busy to start with and therefore it would not be feasible to add to their burdens by giving them administrative responsibilities. For some, this was because assistant pastors had accused them of "passing the buck" in areas that were disliked. For some, it was because the juniors had expressed a disdain for the whole area of administration. And for others, it was a convenient way of keeping all authority in their own hands; for example, in one parish the assistant pastor often did not know until he arose in the morning at what time he would say Mass.

Others, on the contrary, had found it not only easy, but most help-ful to assign duties and seek advice in the area of administration. The following are examples of areas where pastors have expressed satis-faction with the advice given them by assistant pastors in temporali-ties: subdividing rooms in the school; furnishing the library and school; black-topping the parking lot; supervising building fund collections.

One special question of interest in how a pastor might delegate more to his assistant pastors, especially to the more experienced ones, concerned the desirability of establishing a structural change in the parish hierarchy such as a senior position interposed between the pastor and the assistant pastor level. This might be called "Senior Assistant" or "Associate Pastor."[10]

Pastors and assistant pastors were asked about this in the present study. Of the 18 pastors, 4 favored some such structural change, while 13 were against the idea and 1 was doubtful of its wisdom. Of the 15 assistant pastors interviewed, 4 were in favor of the Senior Assistant idea, and 11 were not in favor.

There was general agreement that for all practical purposes in larger parishes one of the assistant pastors actually acted as senior assistant. There was some kind of additional status connected with his work on finances, and an official title would not serve to augment this.

While most agreed that an official title would remove the possibility of a pastor's overburdening himself with these duties by not dele-gating them, there was also a general consensus that it would be better to permit the pastor to give as much or as little of the burden as he wished to whichever assistant pastor he wished. There was a fear that the "wrong man" might be so appointed and thus the pastor would be "saddled" with additional trouble instead of being helped.

Most interviewees felt that the great variety in talents and likes among the priests made it impracticable to establish such a position with uniform duties attached to it. Finally, many thought this would be tantamount to making the position of "clerical business manager" a sort of stepping stone to becoming a pastor, and they felt this would be unfair and unacceptable to most priests. However, there appears to be much sympathy for the idea of some way to increase the motiva-

---

[10] It might be noted that in one diocese at least *all* assistants are termed "Associate Pastors."

tion, even in a material way, for the assistant priest who must, in a large diocese, anticipate up to 20 plus years in the same job position with no additional benefits (salary, fringes) until he becomes a pastor, a move which, for most, comes when they are in their late 40's.

7. *Involving assistant pastors in administrative affairs.* Many younger assistant pastors feel quite strongly that their generation of priests is simply not interested in administration. "You might be surprised to hear this," said one, "but my age bracket of assistant pastors are just not chafing at the bit for the day when they become pastors— they can keep it!" They feel that the use of any priest in the financial administrative areas is a waste of a priest. They are against any priest becoming an "expediter" or procurator.

For a pastor to practice this habit of delegation, therefore, means he will have to accept this antipathy of his assistant pastors for temporalities, and yet do what he can to further their education, if nothing else, in order to prepare them—despite themselves—for assuming these responsibilities at a later time.

In one parish where the income and expenses are just about at the breakeven point, weekly meetings of the priests in the rectory are used to involve all assistant pastors in the administrative affairs of the parish. Attempts are made to keep all informed on the latest plans to keep ahead of the red ink. The inference was that since the financial picture was so tight, it was a good opportunity for the younger priests to pay slightly more attention to this area than they might have otherwise. This is all that is involved in this practice of delegation.

8. *Implementing recent changes in the Church.* In the mind of assistant pastors and lay people, resistance to changes is taken as symptomatic of an underlying resistance to the modernization of the Church, which in turn is viewed as almost synonymous with extending participation in all areas (administrative, liturgical, educational, etc.) to those who before merely followed the dictates of the pastor.

Typical of the non-delegator in this instance was the attitude that "those who rush to make these changes are the hot-shots, the ones trying to leave their footprints in the sands of time."

The response to recent changes in the liturgy and the like is not a question of compliance or lack of compliance. Even the most recalcitrant are obedient. But their people sense it to be a grudging obedience. They take this attitude as symptomatic of being anti-progressive;

and in today's environment this is tantamount to being immoral, for progressiveness has taken on value overtones.

Here too, then, not much more than a willingness to cooperate is all that is involved in this practice of delegation.

9. *Managing by objectives.*   While this phrase was not used with the interviewees, descriptions of the manner in which the pastor assigned or did not assign responsibilities and authority indicated that only five of eighteen could be said to practice anything resembling a system of managing by objectives.

A recurring example of felt lack of leadership lay in the area of the direction to be taken by various parish organizations. Many of them are described as "dying on the vine." The officers go through the motions of their office, but feel the pastor is merely giving lip service to their functions while inwardly wishing the group would "fold up." In most cases the pastors were motivated by a desire not to displease the old-timers belonging to the group. Still, the present officers are put in the position of working for unknown objectives, or at times having their well-meant work undercut by the rectory's subtly downgrading the importance of the group and its goals. A meeting of minds between priests and laymen is definitely called for, to obtain agreement as to the worth of the group, the possibility of changed goals, and the best method to employ to achieve these.

An extreme example of the same lack of agreement on objectives concerning an individual assistant priest was the case of the priest who became aware of his assignment to be responsible for the Confraternity of Christian Doctrine program in the parish (a major assignment for any priest) by reading a notice to that effect posted one day on the rectory bulletin board.

The necessity for plans, goals or objectives in carrying out their duties as priests seemed to escape most of the clergy interviewed, pastors and assistant pastors alike. They seemed to feel they were assigned to maintain some sort of status quo. Still, a few sensed that with such a position should go a desire to achieve some result which could be predetermined. A more analytical approach to optimum use of talents and abilities would help give this sense of direction.

10. *Attempting to overcome the communications gap in the parish.* Eleven of the eighteen pastors thought they were doing something effective to overcome the communications gap, four didn't see there was any, and three saw a problem but had no idea how to cope with it.

When it came to explaining what they were doing to overcome the problem, only eight could point to anything specific, so only these were noted as having this practice of behavior.

Among the things accepted as positive indicators were: suggestion boxes in the church, regular town-hall meetings in the parish hall to air problems, question and answer columns in the parish bulletin, monthly coffee klatches or block meetings attended by different priests in the rectory in different parts of the parish.

This finding also coincides with a major conclusion noted in the priests' survey of 1965 in the subject diocese. The summary report states:

> The section concerned with contacts between the priest and the laity received a 95.1% response from the priests. The general tone of the responses indicates that there is a wall between the priests and the laity. The general attitude in a good number of written responses indicates a resentment to the attitude, evidently not uncommon, of a pastor who looks upon the parish as *his* parish and so sets himself apart from the laity by this very attitude . . . .
>
> Seven out of ten again pointed to the importance of being approachable as a step in the right direction in achieving rapport with the laity. Again it is generally recognized by the reaction to the suggestions that the greatest deterrent to approachableness is the attitude of a pastor who looks upon the parish as *his* and who looks upon the rectory as his castle. Indications of the presence of this attitude are seen in the priest's unwillingness to get out of his rectory and meet the people, or a reluctance to have people come into the rectory.

The nature of the communications problem in the typical parish was described by one interviewee as tantamount to the typical local level of government apathy problem among the public at large. "Just as some town officials have found, we too have discovered that even with regular monthly 'open meetings' of our board, there are very few parishioners who ever show up either to learn anything or to contribute."

Nor are these the only areas where apathy on the part of the majority of members plagues the leaders of groups. The "rank and file" members of many present-day American unions provide the same problem for their leaders: meetings are called and few attend. Beneath the apparent lack of interest in all these groups seems to be one common denominator: the membership does not see how the deliberations affect them. They either do not believe their voice will make any difference in the debates, or they find the deliberative processes move too slowly for all the satisfaction they derive out of playing a role in them. In any case, effort is required to convince them that they do have something to offer, and that something is really sought by the leadership.

At times the people at large understand very little of parish administration. For example some people think all collections are sent to the chancery just as all state taxes are sent to the state capital. One thought that any time his parish runs short of funds, the pastor simply dips into the collection taken up for the diocese. Another thought the parish was at liberty to retain for its purposes any portion it desired of other special collections taken up periodically.

Sometimes the communication problem is just as serious in the rectory as in the parish as a whole. And attempts to overcome this are not always successful. In one parish a routine of regular weekly Monday morning meetings was short-lived and had to be discontinued because they became burdensome and irritating to one of the assistant pastors who had little tolerance for discussion or analysis and preferred more "action."

With regard to the need for greater communication among the priests themselves, the problem was often linked with the broader problem of lack of communication between the individual priest and the bishop of the diocese. It was felt by many that if an assistant pastor had more communication with his bishop, he would find his pastor automatically becoming more communicative. The present "unlimited authority" of the pastor, conjoined with the lack of any check on his behavior or any evaluation system to determine how he exercises his authority, does not provide the motivation needed for close communication between a pastor and his assistant pastors. One suggestion was that the system used by members of religious orders (whereby each person has at least an annual visitation by the provincial superior) might well be adapted by the bishop or his representative.

The younger priests were often critical of the way in which the rectory was called and treated as the priests' house, rather than the parish house. Some felt that opening up the rectory to more visits by members of the parish might help break down the communications barriers. One "avant-garder" suggested that the laity might be invited to a dinner at the rectory now and then so that they might get to know the priests as humans.

The extent of the gulf between what the people know of parish operations and the real facts can be seen in one revealing example. This was the pastor judged by his superiors to be the least efficient of all in financial matters. Yet the pastor himself assessed the situation thus: "I don't talk finances with the people; they tell me: 'It's your baby; you rock it.' They know the parish is in good hands." And true enough, lay persons in the parish felt: "We have an able administrator here. He is open to advice, has much 'savvy' and believes in buying necessary talent to do the job." This appears to be an example of what has been called the "halo effect" in performance evaluation, because a man is judged good in one area (here: spiritual affairs) he is so judged in other areas by his people.

In one parish where there was a modest reserve in the parish bank account, the pastor deliberately withheld this information from the people. He said his key laymen advised this so that the people would not relax and stop contributing. The actual fact of the matter is that the parish in question is fast losing its position as a "wealthy parish" and the reserve will soon be eaten up by rising expenses and dwindling income. But the pastor is "playing the psychological game with the people because I am dependent on them." It is doubtful that he realizes how much of a "sore point" this is with some of his key men.

Hesitancy to overcome the communications gap at times is due to the fear of being labeled a "money priest." Some pastors equate, or think their people equate, discussion of plans and projects of the parish with "dunning the people for money." One of the interviewees is reputed to have taken an oath as a youth never to talk about such things from the pulpit in order not to be a money priest like an old-timer he once was exposed to.

Various pastors are experimenting with different approaches to overcome this communications gap. For example, besides publishing an annual statement of parish income and expenses, some pastors are sending quarterly statements of contributions to all members of the parish, and/or monthly itemizations of all expenses in the Sunday bulletin.

One method used by several pastors is to have periodic general parish meetings in the church hall, where the financial situation and other needs are explained by a team of the priests and influential lay members of the parish. The use of charts, diagrams, budgets, trend-lines, alternative solutions and the like give an air of scientific study to the problems. The emphasis in the discussion is on the need, not on how much money each parish member is expected to contribute.

Beyond the finances area, other parish problems can be better understood and solved only by conscious effort. One method utilizes the "buzz group" approach. After services on Sunday, a copy of the sermon outline is used as the basis for small group discussions over coffee and donuts in the parish hall.

Another singularly effective method being used in some parishes is called the Little Council, which attempts to translate the teachings of Vatican II into the personal and community lives of the parish members. Its purpose usually is to study the Vatican II documents and to open lines of communication between the pastor and his people. It relies on small home discussion groups as a vehicle for interpersonal communication.[11]

A final important way to overcome the communications gap and secure participation is through an informative visit to a newcomer. A brochure is used to explain the way the parish works, and an attempt is made to enlist the aid of the newcomer in his favorite areas of activity through a talent inventory.

II. CONCLUSIONS AND RECOMMENDATIONS

The major conclusion of the above study is that in the area of church administration, as exemplified by the pastors' studies, there is reason to expect a close correlation between a pastor's executive efficiency and the extent to which he practices certain habits of delegation to competent lay advisors and/or assistant pastors in a line or staff capacity.

In addition, the following important conclusions can be stated:

1. Backgrounds make some difference.
2. Size of parish makes some difference.
3. Managerial concepts and principles are not understood.
4. Time is allocated inefficiently.
5. Pastors reflect delegation they perceive in their own superiors.
6. There is a lack of performance criteria.
7. There is lack of development assistance.
8. There is little use of true budgets.

[11] Cf. "Little Council at St. Bede's," *Michigan Catholic*, 2/9/67.

1. *Backgrounds make some difference.* With regard to backgrounds of pastors, younger and newer pastors could be expected to practice a greater degree of delegation and apparently do. Older men who practice higher amounts of delegation tend to have been trained that way in earlier administrative positions.

Because of the inverse relationship between a pastor's age and his ability—or desire—to improve efficiency through the practice of greater delegation, it seems reasonable to set a limit on the age at which a pastor can continue in office.

Great caution must be used in arbitrarily lowering the age limit and rigidly enforcing new rules like these, at least for a while. This for two very important reasons. First, the age cannot be lowered too far too fast owing to the lack of priests to fill the vacancies that will be created. Second, and more important: this is still a new concept for clergymen. It must be implemented prudently and carefully. It would be injudicious, to say the least, if a senior pastor who has given the better part of his life to his parish, literally making of his parishioners his family (for he has no other), were to be cut off and thrown away like an old shoe. Provision must be made for him to continue his apostolic works, relieving him only of his administrative cares, and providing him with suitable retirement pension.

2. *Size of parish makes some difference.* With regard to the parishes the pastors serve, larger parishes (2000 families and up) and those in higher income areas tend to require greater delegation from their pastors. The makeup of the parish is a constraint on how the pastor must administer. The business-oriented parish demands more detailed accounting of, and participation in, plans, programs and expenditures. These same parishes can afford to hire many services such as payroll and insurance, bookkeeping, recording of contributions and the like. In these parishes there seems no problem in getting money when needed, except for operating expenses; so that the pastor does not even "feel" heavily burdened by administrative duties.

Because of the scarcity of priests and rising costs in duplicating many buildings, the best solution might be found in smaller parishes (one priest only) with fewer buildings and material problems so that the pastor would have more time for spiritual matters. A number of small parishes could feed a few central schools staffed by professionals. Cutting back on physical plants would eliminate the necessity for much administrative work, while fewer families would mean greater chance of personal contact with the pastor. Younger priests could receive their training in a few large central parishes and staff offices.

Many today feel there is a tendency to put too much money into the buildings themselves. The elaborateness of some parish plants is viewed as a pastor's testimonial to his own encumbency, even though very often this is actually farthest from his mind. Perhaps the emphasis should be on functionalism rather than on beauty.

3. *Managerial concepts and principles are not understood.* There is much confusion regarding the meaning of such basic concepts as authority, responsibility and control. The low delegators hesitate to use their advisors because they do not understand how to relinquish authority and yet maintain control; how to rid themselves of details without surrendering controls.

Many pastors are simply creatures of their earlier environment. It is difficult if not impossible for a man who has been "a country pastor for 25 years" to be comfortable with what he perceives as "fancy big-time goings-on." It might be helpful for such men to analyze what is going on under the fancy trappings they fear. For example, Robert Tannenbaum's simple division of the decision-making process into four logical steps might appeal to them: *a*) the recognition of the problem in all its aspects; *b*) the analysis of alternatives and their consequences; *c*) the logical conclusion concerning the most acceptable of the alternatives; *d*) the executive order that this alternative rather than any other is to be put into effect. It is only in the last step that authority is called into play.[12]

The members of a council or advisory board do not share in the authority of the bishop or pastor from the point of view of decision-making, but the very purpose of their office and function is to share in the responsibilities of management. The extent to which their contribution is necessary depends partly on the size and complexity of the organization. In a simple culture where the apostolic works of the Church were routinized and where the functions demanded little specialization, the preliminary steps to decision probably required little consultation.

[12] Robert Tannenbaum, "Managerial Decision-Making," *Journal of Business,* Vol. 23, No. 1 (Jan. 1950), pp. 22–39; also "The Manager Concept—A Rational Synthesis," *Journal of Business,* Vol. 22, No. 4 (Oct. 1949), pp. 209–241.

Especially for those who might feel uncomfortable with their new sharing of their authority, perhaps the following could serve as a program for beginning to delegate more:

a) "Make haste slowly" is an old ecclesiastical proverb. Today's pastor should not rush pell-mell to join the bandwagon for the "emergence of the layman" or any other single program. Many laymen don't really know much about their Church. Liberalism and progressiveness will not inevitably follow the delegation of more responsibility to the laity. As a matter of fact, if a certain element gains control, a parish could go backward overnight. The Church needs leadership with vision and this is not necessarily identified with the laity.

b) Two necessities are a parish council to share the decision-making responsibilities and a parish budget.

c) Then the parish should be properly staffed through preplanning and design. The role of the parish should be clearly defined. Once the pastor knows where he is going, he can get there in stages. Priorities should be established, keeping in mind that the ordained priest's first duty is religious. He should endeavor to reserve for himself the duties requiring his talents and training.

d) Assignment of duties to others in the parish should be done using a system such as management by objectives. But, whether this or any other system of management is used, the place to start is with the question: What is a parish for? rather than: What should we change?

Further, in making assignments, the pastor should recall he is there for a specific purpose: that within the context of saving souls he is sent to a specific place with specific problems, and he should make sure he and his assistant pastors have a clear understanding of the nature of those specific problems and how to combat them.

4. *Time is allocated inefficiently.* A fundamental problem of modern-day parochial life remains: How can the pastor find the optimum division of his limited time between spiritual duties and the more mundane temporal matters of administration? Most interviewees in this research were convinced it was a matter of "freeing" the priest from administrative trivia. Some of this could be done by proper use of paid or volunteer clerical help. More than this is required today. The message of Vatican II as understood by those

interviewed was simple: "Involve the layman in the operation of the parish; utilize his talents; enlist his cooperation to free the priest for priestly functions."

This seems to call for a restructuring of the parish. Further research must investigate in depth the attempts being made now to find workable new patterns of authority and delegation through the use of parish councils, school boards, paid business managers, administrative teams of pastors, not so much as a way of curbing the authority of pastors, but as ways of reassigning responsibilities in a parish according to the special talents and preparation of all its members.

Jay W. Forrester suggests, in order to depart from the authoritarian hierarchy as the central organizational structure, that one replace the superior-subordinate pair as the fundamental building block in the organization. He describes the fluid relationship that Bennis envisions:

> In the new organization an individual would not be assigned to a superior. Instead he would negotiate, as a free individual, a continually changing structure of relationships with those with whom he exchanges goods and services. He would accept specific obligations as agreements of limited duration. As these are discharged, he would establish a new pattern of relationships as he finds more satisfying and rewarding situations.[13]

This study has identified a superior-subordinate relationship (that of the pastor and assistant pastor) which is ready-made for the use of such a concept, and shown how the various priests' desire for a more equalitarian attitude between pastor and assistant pastor, such as is forecast by Forrester, would help the overall efficiency of the parish.

5. *Pastors reflect the delegation they perceive in their own superiors.* In many ways the attitude and consequent behavior of the pastor toward his advisors and assistant pastors is a reflection of his attitude toward his superiors and how much delegation they practice.

Studies in industry have shown how futile it is to train first-line supervisors in "good human relations" or any other facet of leadership, unless one can be sure the trained supervisor will be put back into a situation where the leadership climate above him is conducive

---

[13] Jay W. Forrester, "A New Corporate Design," *Industrial Management Review*, Fall, 1965.

to the practice of the skills he has sharpened.[14] Hence the stress in training today that leadership styles must be adopted at the highest echelons first, before they can expect to meet with successful application at the lower levels of supervision. In the present context, the pastor is akin to a first-line supervisor. He is only acting as he would be expected to act if he follows the pattern of what he sees being practiced by his own administrative superiors.

6. *There is a lack of performance criteria.*   There are few criteria which are used by either pastor or his superiors to measure the performance of the pastor. His efficiency all too frequently is estimated only in the financial areas. Among most pastors who have given thought to what the norms for a successful pastor might be, the main emphasis centered on this matter of the financial picture of the parish. This they resented. They felt they had not been trained to "keep books" or manage a school or purchase supplies, yet they were judged on how they materially managed a parish. There is need for further study to establish norms for measuring a pastor's administrative ability. This might be made a part of the current attempt to study and determine the true role of the pastor, the religious and the laity in the modern parish.

There are few guidelines for the pastor to use in meeting his responsibilities. He is almost always assigned to a parish without benefit of clear-cut instructions as to what he is expected to accomplish, or the reason—if any—for his being given that particular assignment. An objective approach in making the assignment of the pastor would help him in planning, delegating and carrying out his duties.

7. *There is lack of development assistance.*   There are no guidelines for pastors to practice self-development. There is a general feeling among priests that since this is not covered in any formal education they receive, they are perforce expected to improve their administrative abilities from discussion, from on the job training, from observing it being done by others. "A process of osmosis" it is called by some. Others prefer a series of clergy conferences, though many

[14] Cf. Edwin A. Fleishman, "Leadership Climate, Human Relations Training and Supervisory Behavior" in Fleishman, editor, *Studies in Personnel and Industrial Psychology* (Homewood, Illinois: The Dorsey Press, Inc., 1961), pp. 315–328.

find they are so busy with routine duties that they simply cannot take time to attend the conferences that are held on other aspects of the pastor's work. Most of those interviewed, despite the necessity of their keeping themselves advised of recent changes in Church law, theology, etc., seem to find it impossible to adopt a suitable program of self-study in administrative matters.

They find solace in the fact that in their type of community life, where they not only work together, but also live together under the same roof, they just have to learn something from each other over the years, short of the rare times when a pastor will deliberately hide administrative matters from the younger priests.

8. *There is little use of true budgets.*   There is little understanding of, or appreciation for, the use of budgets in the management of a parish. In most cases any dislike of a budget appears to come from wrong ideas as to how they work. One pastor said he preferred to say he did not have a budget, because to him the whole concept of budget meant a ceiling. He preferred to work with what he called a "plan or forecast of income and expenses." His explanation really indicated he hoped for a fluctuating budget, and he actually was operating with one whether he chose to call it such or not.

Those who tend to shy away from the use of a budget and its implications are those who fear the perspicacity of their men. These are the ones who tend to rely more on the women's groups in the parish as the strong lay groups. "The men ask questions about how the money is spent when they give it. The women don't ask questions."

One important aspect of budgeting neglected in almost every parish was the area of depreciation or any funding for maintenance or replacement. Traditionally the concern of all seems to be on how to provide for today's expenses and how to pay off the debt—not necessarily in that order! If replacement or expansion needs occur later, more borrowing will be done (very often at a higher rate of interest), or the expense will be met by special collections or special fund-raising activities. This is why the church often becomes, according to one pastor, a "bingo-playing, raffle-giving church," when the money should be put aside in advance.

When this happens, the means become the end or at least become a necessity. For example, some bingo and athletic programs are the main source of income, so much time and energy are put into them.

This in turn leads to "bingo priests" or "jock-strap Christianity."

Current diocesan regulations regarding financial reporting could be expanded and deepened to include guidelines for the preparation and use of budgets. Some improvements in this direction are being made now in the attempt to break school expenses out of total parish expenses.

CHAPTER NINE

A CASE STUDY

As we approach the end of our study of the priest-manager, it might be helpful to examine in detail some of the opportunities a typical priest-manager might have to put into practice the principles we have examined. There may be those who feel it will be time enough to do this after diocesan and parish structures have been reorganized to do away with many of the administrative chores the average parish priest now has. But this may take a little time in some instances, and it would be a shame for the reader to do nothing meanwhile to improve his managerial patterns.

It seems appropriate, therefore, to study some of the present activities of the typical parish priest to recognize what he should *not* do and ask what he might now do on his own without waiting for new structures. To do this we shall take a day in the life of a busy metropolitan pastor, though we could just as well have chosen a chancery official or a school administrator. The man we shall study is not personally known to the writer, but he will be recognized by the reader, because he embodies something of many priests, all rolled into one. In a word, he is a fictitious person, yet acts realistically, exemplifying many who are in the same position as he.

The detailed examination of such a hypothetical person in a series of hypothetical situations is a "case study." Such cases are frequently used as vehicles for learning, especially in management courses or workshops. It should not be necessary to point out that the delineation of character in such a case is in no way meant to ridicule individuals or groups of individuals. The picture we get of our fictitious pastor is neither an indictment nor a model. It is drawn merely to afford an opportunity to view objectively an actor in a life-like situation and to analyze his behavior in order to learn from it. The usual case study allows the reader to discuss pros and cons and does not itself take a position. For those who would want to do that with this chapter, we preface our case with some discussion questions which should be kept in mind while reading the case. At the end of the case, we shall single out certain events for special comment in relation to principles discussed in earlier chapters.

"The Spirit Indeed Is Willing . . ."[1]

Discussion Questions:
    i. What is the major problem in this case? Be very specific in stating it. Whose problem is it?
    ii. What might be the underlying causes of this problem?
    iii. Can you think of any possible courses of action that might be taken to solve this problem (cause eliminators)?
    iv. What would you suggest be done? By whom? Why?

It was approximately 7:45 Tuesday morning when Father Tom Putoff, pastor of St. Raphael's parish, stepped out the rear door from the sacristy into the morning sun. It was a beautiful early June day. A cool, fresh breeze was blowing. On mornings like this, Father Tom especially enjoyed his daily ten minute walk around the parish property which had become his custom after he completed his thanksgiving after Mass.

St. Raphael's was a "big city parish," located in a still growing suburb. Most of its 1800 or so families were of the lower or upper middle class social strata, with a number of aggressive "executives" and also a fair share of skilled and semi-skilled workers.

The parish had just celebrated the fifteenth anniversary of its founding, and clergy and lay alike were justifiably proud of how complete a parish plant had been built and paid for—or almost paid for—in those fifteen years. Father Tom had personally seen to the laying of every brick and the planting of every shrub as the
[1] buildings and property took shape. This was truly his parish, which he, and his parishioners, had raised from the empty field that first greeted his arrival the day the bishop had "sent me out in the country to take care of the expanding population in the area."

As the morning sun glittered on the Italian stained glass win-
[2] dows lining the rear of the sanctuary, Father Tom began his daily ten minute "inspection tour" that would take him around the new church, grade school, parish meeting hall and convent, across the paved parking lot, and finally back to the rear door of the rectory where good old Mrs. McCartney was preparing the poached egg breakfast she said his easily upset stomach should have.

[1] Originally printed in *Homiletic and Pastoral Review*, Jan. 1968. Reprinted by permission of publisher, John F. Wagner, Inc., New York.

Father Tom stepped briskly on the pavement, thinking of the many duties facing him this day. In the fresh air he always did his best planning. "On such a glorious day," he thought to himself, "this is really going to be a day to get things done." He began to [3] run through the day's work, first one project then another, trying to establish priorities. After a few minutes he decided that preparing next Sunday's sermon was probably high on the list. Hearing the comments of several members of the parish about the "down-to-earth" sermons of his two Assistants had made the pastor reflect that it had been a long time since someone had said that about his homilies. Maybe an earlier start in the week on outlining the sermon would help. This he must start today.

Then there was that matter of reorganizing the various organizations in the parish. This had been the subject of quite some dis- [4] cussion with the ushers as they sat around for their usual bottle of beer after the week's offertory collection had been counted in the [5] rectory last evening. Paul Needler, principal of the local high school, was always one to vocalize what a lot of his fellow laymen only thought to themselves.

For about the ninth time Paul had asked Father Tom when he was going to outline to him and the other members of the Church Committee just what their duties were. "Don't get me wrong, [6] Father," Paul had said. "We all enjoy coming over for cocktails and dinner every year right after New Year's, but I understand some parishes ask their committee to do more than sign the annual report. This seems to be one area where the Vatican Council expects us to do something."

Father Tom had answered, as on the other times when the subject had come up, that he heartily agreed with this idea. "As you know, Paul, it has always been my policy to utilize to the maximum the abilities of you laymen. And we were doing that long [7] before Vatican II ever convened. Why this whole plant was erected with the officers of the Ushers Club approving every decision I made. That's why I am so careful to be sure to pick the right men to be on the Church Committee. You people are specially trained in areas we priests know nothing about. If we put down in black and white all the ways you help me, you'd see how progressive we really are."

It was easy to recall his answer: he had said it so often. He [8] had really intended to get to work on this reorganization for about a year now, but something always seemed to crop up. "I haven't had much time to sit down and really work it out," he said to himself. "I'd better get going and really hit this one today for sure."

A honk from a passing car broke into his thoughts, and he recognized Jim Foresight, loan officer at a suburban bank, waving as he turned the corner on his way to the office. "There's one banker who doesn't work banker's hours," mused Father Tom. He had always admired Jim's ability to plan and organize. As a matter of fact, he missed Jim's participation in the parish building campaign. He had been a natural to head up the committee as replacement for poor Dan Mixup after that terrible accident. Jim had been in the parish only six months before Dan's death, and it was a stroke of fate that he literally bumped into Father Tom making a [9]   deposit one day right after Dan's funeral. The chance meeting included an offer by Jim to help in any way he could in the parish. So Father had asked him on the spot to drop in and discuss this committee job.

"That's what I mean by using laymen according to their ability," thought Father. And Jim would have been great too. Unfortunately, after several weeks of conferences and plans and alternate proposals to reorganize the campaign procedures in a way that would meet the requirements of other parish organizations as Father patiently explained them to Jim, it became necessary for [10]   Jim to put in extra hours at the bank, so he reluctantly resigned as committee chairman. "I must try to finalize those plans we were working on," thought Father Tom. "It's been two months now, and there's only three more months left before we begin our collection effort again after Labor Day. . . . Yes, sir, this is the day to really get rolling!"

Father's thoughts were interrupted as he entered the rectory rear door by the jangle of the telephone. He was closest to the phone in the hallway, so he answered it cheerfully, "St. Raphael's; good morning; Father Putoff speaking."

"Oh, Father, I'm glad you're not out on a Communion visit." It [11]   was the eighth grade Sister calling, very distraughtly. "You know today is the day for individual and group pictures of the graduating eighth graders . . . and the man is due here in 15 minutes . . . and Mrs. Lately was supposed to come in an hour early before her duties in the school office to help arrange the children and record who was who and take orders and all . . . and it appears she can't make it after all . . . and so we will need a lady from the parish to help . . . and will you get us someone please?"

"Now Sister," said Father calmly. "Don't fret. We've still got fifteen minutes. If I've told you once, I've told you a dozen times. The parish is full of good people who would be happy to come over for a couple of hours to help out. All I have to do is call. You get back to your preparations and I'll have someone there in 30 minutes at most."

Fifteen minutes later Father sat down to a cold poached egg, [12]   explaining to Mrs. McCartney that her friend Mrs. Reliable had once again agreed to come over and lend a helping hand. She had been the fourth parishioner called. The first two were busy signals. The third lady unfortunately had a dentist's appointment, but if

Father wished she would come by after the appointment to help out. And why would that be too late—the children would be at school all day wouldn't they? Oh, it was the photographer who wouldn't be there all day. Well, if Father wanted her to call her dentist and change the appointment, she'd be only too glad to. Father didn't want her to do that? Well, if Father preferred someone else. . . .

Finishing his second cup of coffee, Father lit another cigarette and headed for his desk in the front office. Today was Father Bright's day off (Senior Assistant) and Father Young was tied up at the high school this morning (Junior Assistant and part-time student counsellor at the nearby Central Catholic High School). So Father Tom was going to work in the front office this morning as he always did whenever his two Assistants were away.

[13] This was because of a rule he insisted on: there must always be a priest in the office area to render quickly any service required by the people. Too many parishes made the people wait and wait while the housekeeper or bookkeeper sought a priest from the mysterious interior regions of the rectory. Here at St. Raphael's there would be no such delays. Here we were better organized than that. Here there was always a priest available almost at once. We prided ourselves on being readily accessible to the people. That's why there was no such thing as office hours and signs requesting the people not to ring the bell during meal time, etc. A priest has to be available 24 hours a day!

[14] Drawing his chair up to the desk, Father saw the pile of checks he had been in the process of signing the evening before when he had to leave them half undone in order to meet with the money-counting team of ushers. The one on top had really made him livid last evening and now would be a good time to straighten that matter out. It was just a little after 9 o'clock and that Lawn Service Company should be open.

[15] Dialing the number, he tried to recall what that radio commercial had said. "For a lawn that rivals your favorite golfing greens! . . . I distinctly remember telling your truck driver that I'd be surprised if this works, because we had tried so much before, but he guaranteed me that your treatment would make our lawn the envy of the neighborhood. . . . What do you mean it will take more than two applications because we had so many weeds? . . . I insist you come out and inspect this situation personally. . . . Very well, I'll expect you at two this afternoon. Good bye."

[16] Feeling very good about not having to pay that bill just yet, Father Tom continued through the pile of checks to be signed, very carefully comparing the amount on the check with the amount on the attached invoice, and noting with pride the initials of Mrs. Tight, the bookkeeper who was now going on 15 years of

faithful service, morning after morning. Mrs. Tight hadn't made an error in preparing checks in her entire 15 years. She was so dependable that when the pastor took his annual vacation, he merely signed several blank checks and left them in her care to pay the necessary bills, and she always accounted properly for each one upon his return.

[17]   What was this one? Five dollars and thirty-two cents out of the Altar Society account for ice cream used at the annual elections meeting two weeks ago. But Mrs. Speaker, the Sodality President (until September) had said Mr. Softouch at the corner drug store was donating that ice cream. The women always work hard to keep expenses down and made it a point to get the ice cream from Mr. Softouch. They felt the parish should patronize his store because he buys the largest advertisement in the parish bulletin. "I wonder what happened. . . ."

[18]   An hour and ten minutes later Father put down the telephone, having obtained the explanation from Mrs. Speaker. He was also now better informed on which of the new officers really should not have been elected; on the terrible affront she had personally felt when the incoming Sodality President had omitted to mention two of the eight new projects begun during the last year in her assignment of committee appointments; on the possibility that one of the staunch members of the parish might actually be encouraging other ladies in the parish to join the WOVDM, the "We Object to Vietnam Demonstration March" next week; and on several other choice items.

[19]   Just at that moment Mrs. Tight (who had arrived a little while earlier) came into the office with the mail which she carefully deposited in the appropriate in-basket on Father's desk. But before Father Tom could slice open a single one of the many envelopes, he realized it was 11 o'clock and the ring at the front door was probably Carl Anxious who was always most prompt to keep his weekly appointment for his marriage instruction.

[20]   The hour long discussion with Carl was interrupted twice: once by a salesman who dropped by to leave Father Tom a sample of a new floor wax he was trying to get Father to use on the church and school floors; the second time by a phone call from the school
[21]   office asking Father Tom when the protective guard rail for the broken bicycle rack in the rear of the school would be installed.

"What broken bicycle rack?" he asked, surprised by the question.

"The one near the parking lot which someone must have run over sometime during the afternoon classes yesterday. There were four bicycles seriously damaged and the rack itself is now useless."

"Why wasn't I notified when it happened?"

"I don't know, Father," said Sister Superior. "I was discussing it with the custodian last evening and he said the insurance would take care of everything, so I thought you knew about it."

"What did you say he wants to do?"

"He said he would build a 4 inch protective metal rail around the rack. I thought he had your permission the way he was talking. I'm sorry if I assumed. . . ."

"That's all right, Sister. Thank you for advising me. But please tell Mr. Leftout not to do anything until I examine his plan."

[22] By the time Carl left, it was noon, and the housekeeper was announcing lunch. Father Young had returned from school, and he joined the pastor for a light noon meal. Neither had much to inform the other about—they actually worked in such different worlds that it was difficult to discuss much in common except recent changes in regulations regarding the breviary, etc.

Excusing himself from the table, Father Tom hurried back into the office to get at that unopened mail. No sooner had he glanced at all the return addresses and selected the envelope from the diocesan school office as the first one to open when the door bell rang again. Soon one of the high school girls (who had arrived to relieve Mrs. Tight at 12:30) appeared to announce a lady was here to see him.

"Can Father Young take care of her?" asked Father.

"She asked for the pastor," replied the teenager.

"All right. Show her in please."

[23] After two minutes Mrs. Fussbudget came into the office, apologizing for interrupting Father Tom. "I'm so sorry to bother you, Father. I know how busy you are. But I'd like a Mass said for my dear departed husband, and you know I always like you to say it personally. So I came in early so you could put this Mass on your calendar for November 10th for sure."

Ten minutes later, as Father ushered Mrs. Fussbudget to the front door, he thought to himself, "If only I could train these girls how to handle callers like this one. But I guess that's part of the [24] price I have to pay for voluntary help. And it's a small price to pay considering how much the parish has saved in secretarial wages. Guess that's my contribution to a cost consciousness program. . . ."

The letter from the school office was just another one of those reminders that teachers for the next year would expect to be enrolled in the new diocesan-wide employees insurance retirement [25] program. "They have some nerve," thought Father, "spending my money for me. I suppose one of these days I'll have to call a meeting of our lay teachers and explain this program to them. . . ."

None of the other mail was very interesting, except for an advertisement about some new school desks that looked rather [26] nice. "That's something I must ask Fr. Pat Oldtimer about, over at St. Mary's tonight at the Forty Hours dinner. I hear he's tried a few of these. . . ."

And then one of the girls was announcing the arrival of a Mr.

Green. "He must be a bill collector or something, Father, because
[27]   when I asked him what it was about, he said he wanted to explain
why you should pay a bill or something. . . ."

Whereupon Father Tom thanked her and ushered Mr. Green
outside to have a look at the lawn. . . .

During the last half hour before he had to leave for the Forty
Hours dinner, Father Tom was able to return to his desk. He
thought he would make another stab at trying to reorganize the
parish structure. He had meant it the preceding night when he
told the men he would work on this. Why, he *had* been working
at it. He reached in his desk and took out the rough notes he had
sketched so far of what a parish organization chart might look like.
Ever since he had heard that management talk a year ago in which
the speaker recommended that all organizations should have a
drawn organization chart, Father Tom had been working on one
[28]   for St. Raphael. Once again, then, he took it out and looked at it.
(See Figure 21 for replica of incomplete chart). As he examined
his notes, he wondered what the next step should be. . . . The
more he looked at it, the more he wondered, and the more he
smoked. . . . Before he knew it, it was time to leave and reluctantly he put away his notes until another time.

As he drove out of the garage, Father Tom reflected on what
had been accomplished during the day, especially regarding the
two projects he had intended to get at: Sunday's sermon and
parish organization. "At least," he thought ruefully, "I worked for
a half hour on the second one. . . ."

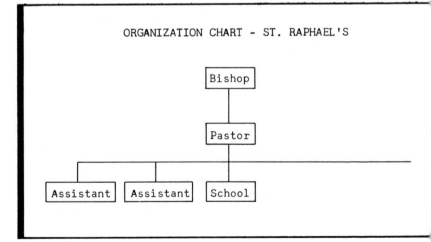

FIGURE 21

Case Analysis

Someone with nothing better to do one day discovered no less than 53 separate points in the foregoing case which can be used to illustrate some management point. To cover that many here would take too long—and not be necessarily helpful either. The following discussion points have been keyed to the appropriate paragraphs in the case. They follow in sequence from the beginning of the case.

[1] After locating our hero, Fr. Tom Putoff, in a middle class suburban parish fifteen years old, we get a glimpse of his attitude toward this parish. It is "his" parish, which he birthed, nurtured and developed brick by brick, shrub by shrub. Besides the obvious preconciliar notion that a parish is a collection of physical assets, what can be said about his "personally seeing to the laying of every brick," etc.? Is this the work of the priest? Is this an area where he might delegate the personal supervision of work to someone else? Can an architect be convinced this is part of his responsibility? Can a parishioner, knowledgeable in these things, check up on construction workers and landscapers? Can Father Tom fulfill his responsibility (meaning accountability here) to the bishop and his people without personally babying along the project?

[2] We see Father on this early June morning making an "inspection tour" of ten minute duration. Is this a commendable practice? If he never does it, can he keep fully aware of how the parish is going? If he believes the physical plant is not what he should be spending his time on, can he ignore it completely?

[3] Father's mind is busy reviewing the day's work, trying to establish priorities. Is this a good practice? Is this the kind of planning of time mentioned earlier as a proper way to allocate this precious resource? Can Father Tom do this at the same time he is trying to make an inspection tour, or is this an example of doing two commendable things in a way which hurts both?

[4] Our pastor recalls what happened the evening before as he was with the men who were having a bottle of beer after counting the weekly collection. Should the pastor be with the men that way? Should he himself help count the money, or would that be a waste of his talents? Could he be there to police the activity, because it's been known to happen that some of the collection found its way to other

accounts than the parish's? Can his presence with this group of presumably dedicated parishioners serve a valuable function if he were to take the opportunity to use them as "sounding boards"?

[5] Is there any significance in the high school principal's name—Needler?

[6] What's bothering Needler is the fact that apparently all the Church Committee does is gather once a year for a little holiday cheer and to sign a report. Is this the function of a Church Committee? If the letter of the law requires only a signature on a report, is this the idea behind it? What responsible laymen would today just come over and sign something they know next to nothing about?

[7] Father's stock answer—he knew it by rote now—was to point out how he had used participative management and decision-making for a long time. Why, the men approved every decision *he made*. Is this the right concept of participation? Is this really stealing a march on Vatican II? In picking the "right men" for the committee, did he look for a variety of views or those he knew would agree with his own?

[8] Apparently our hero recognizes he is having trouble getting around to parish reorganization. He has been trying to get to it for a year now, but "something always seemed to crop up." How long do we struggle with something, especially something foreign to our training and personal inclination, before we get help? Does it sound as though he will ever get to it? Is something always cropping up a sure sign of our ability, or inability, to tackle a job and see it through?

[9] We are then introduced, through Father Tom's reverie, to Jim Foresight. And almost parenthetically we learn how the two men met. It was on the occasion of one of the pastor's trips to the bank to deposit the Sunday's collection. Whose job should that be?

[10] What about the circumstances leading to Foresight's resignation from the fund-raising committee? Wasn't it too bad that he had to work late nights and could not help any more? Or is it possible lay people might sometimes become "unavailable" when they feel they have had just about enough "patient explanation"?

[11] The next event is the telephone conversation with the eighth grade Sister regarding help for student picture-taking. Is this the sort of thing that must be brought to the attention of the pastor? Doesn't this poor teacher know that the pastor is a busy man and can't she handle any of her own problems? Or could it be that people act according to the way their leaders train them? It is possible that delega-

tion can be seen or not seen in the way people act? Is the pastor's immediate response—to call around to get help—a sign of how he delegates?

[12] We find that Father Tom succeeds in enlisting the aid of a Mrs. Reliable. Why is she called that? Has Father learned after fifteen years anything about getting volunteer help?

[13] We quickly pass over mention of what Father has for breakfast and skip the chance of speculating on what might cause his stomach to be easily upset. We also omit comment on the names of the two assistants (or their titles), and move on to consider the rationale for Father Tom to now have to spend the morning in the front office. As he explains it to us, he is willing to put in his time, as it were, because of his strong conviction that the priests at St. Raphael's must be readily accessible. Just how much should this conviction be pushed? Is he correct in banning signs about office hours? Would people resent a request not to disturb the priests during meal hours? Just what does "available 24 hours" mean? Can people be taught the difference between routine office hours kinds of things and other more serious matters? Do we want our lay people to feel the rectory is their house as much as the priests', so they should feel free to drop in at any time just as they would to a neighbor's house, since we form a big "community"?

[14] The first task our busy pastor undertakes is the signing of some checks left over from the previous day. This raises the question: who should sign checks? Who is authorized by diocesan regulations to be a signer? How many names—and whose—should be on the signature cards at the bank? Can anyone but the pastor have power of attorney? Can some distinction be made between routine expenditures and exceptional items?

[15] Then comes the matter of the Green Acres Lawn Service. Who ought to be spending his time with such matters? What if it is impossible to find custodial/maintenance personnel qualified to look after major elements of the parish plant? What about the ad which prompted the pastor to call this service in the first place? Is there any truth to the suggestion whispered *sotto voce* at conventions that priests generally make a good "sucker list"? Are there ways in which to protect oneself against such "come-on's"?

[16] The check signing continues, a careful comparison being made between the prepared check and the corresponding invoice,

which we learn has all been done by Mrs. Tight, the bookkeeper. Apparently she has been delegated the responsibility of preparing the checks, and her work is being carefully scrutinized. After 15 years of such scrutinizing, she hasn't yet been caught in error. How long should Father keep carefully checking her work? Or is it just a game to see if he can catch her? Is there any connection between this point and the earlier check signing issue?

[17] Then the ice cream invoice from Mr. Softouch comes to light. There must be a mistake: he always donates the refreshments. We patronize his store because he buys an ad in the church paper. How many other patrons of the same type will it take to put him out of business?

[18] To find out what happened, there transpires a 70 minute phone conversation with Mrs. Speaker. Is it possible Father had to listen to her that long in order not to insult her? Or is it possible that the phone can become a "security blanket," the only way we have of feeling we are busy and keeping in touch with things? Is this the way to get to the items on the priority list for the day?

[19] When the mail is brought in, Father Tom hardly has time to slice open a single letter when the door bell rings to announce Carl Anxious, the groom-to-be. Wonder why the opening of mail's done by the pastor personally. Is he fearful that some correspondence might be confidential and therefore even faithful Mrs. Tight should not be allowed to see it? Or is it possible to train a trusted employee to sort out the matters of conscience, should there be any? Does Father ever dictate answers on these confidential matters, or is that a different story completely?

[20] The first interruption in Carl's marriage instruction concerned a wax salesman. Who should be talking to such a person? Can we delegate purchasing, or at least demonstrations, of supply items to janitorial personnel?

[21] The second interruption was a phone call from the school office about a broken bicycle rack. How did our hero happen to miss this during his morning inspection tour which took him right past it? The decision here is to do nothing until Father has a chance to examine the custodian's plan to place a four inch protective rail around the rack. Apparently Mr. Leftout is just exactly that. . . .

[22] Lunch time finds the pastor and Fr. Young with very little to talk about. It appears they live in two different worlds. Is this an

opportunity to try to overcome the artificial barriers separating two generations of priests? How assiduously is it used? It is often said that staff meetings are not necessary in a rectory "because after all we live together and see each other at least at meal times and talk things over then". . . .

[23] Back in the office after lunch, Father receives Mrs. Fussbudget. Apparently it was a routine matter of scheduling a Mass for some five months hence, and the pastor thinks longingly of training the girls to handle such callers. Is it possible to do this? Can an intelligent receptionist learn to sort out the serious matters from the routine? Can you ask a parishioner not to call on the busy priests without an appointment, as is done for other professionals and executives (barring emergencies) or is that now against the Vatican idea of community? How do you provide for the penitent who walks up and down in front of the rectory for a long time mustering up courage to see the priest and who outwardly might appear to be on routine business (a Mass stipend) only to let open the flood gates once inside the private office of the priest?

[24] Father Tom's reason for not hiring a secretary—his cost consciousness—deserves special consideration. Is there any validity in his position; that he is trying to do his share, carefully conserving the people's money by not hiring someone? Or would the lay people be the first ones to feel this is being penny wise but pound foolish, given all the things the priest cannot do because he lacks secretarial help?

[25] The letter from the school office stipulating that teachers be enrolled in a retirement program touches a sensitive nerve. Apparently Father doesn't like this business of diocesan officials—down at Thrush central—spending his money for him. What is the extent of a pastor's control of parish funds? How much authority should diocesan offices have in demanding certain personnel procedures and policies? Is there a parallel here with what a local plant manager might be called on to do as a member of a large corporation? Or do those things apply only in the business world?

[26] An ad about some school desks attracts the pastor's eye. Something to check out with Fr. Oldtimer at Forty Hours. This is undoubtedly a good place to begin in checking out the desks since he apparently has some first hand experience with them. Where else can Father go to check them out? Should he check further? Has he learned to develop other sources than his clergy friends?

[27] Mr. Green, the lawn service man, arrives and we see how our volunteer girls handle visitors again. The teenager thinks he's a bill collector or something. Wouldn't Father have a stroke if he heard the conversation at the dinner table that evening when the teenager went home? Asked by her mother, if there was anything new going on at the rectory, the youngster might say, "Oh, not much. We did the usual work. But there was one thing: I think Father Putoff is in some kind of trouble because this man came to see him, and he said it was about why Father should pay a bill or something, and then they went outside to talk about it: I guess they didn't want any of us to hear. . . ."

[28] Finally, before it was time to leave the rectory to attend a Forty Hours ceremony, Father took out the work papers he had on the parish organization chart, wondering what to do about it. And the more he looked at it, the more he wondered and the more he wondered, the more he smoked; and after a half-hour he reluctantly put his "work" away. Father summarizes his day's work on his two priority items: "At least I worked for a half-hour on the second one." Did he?

What do we think of Fr. Putoff as an administrator? Is he working hard? Undoubtedly, with an easily upset stomach to prove it. Is he doing a good job? Judged by parish buildings, reductions of debt and the like, he appears to have made much progress in fifteen years. (We aren't given any information about the spiritual state of his parish.) Is he endeavoring to keep his eye on everything and provide the kinds of services he thinks his people need? Admittedly, he is even trying to organize his time and concentrate on priority items. We saw him try to do this from the very start of his busy day. But what happened? Despite his willingness to concentrate on priority items, something always seemed to come up. Perhaps the title of this little vignette gives us a clue. Perhaps it's a matter of wanting to do things the way modern techniques say we should, but just not being able to because we are creatures of habit. Perhaps in administrative matters, as in spiritual, it's a matter of the spirit being willing, but. . . .